Your Own Business in Europe
How to Branch Out or Start Up a New Business in Europe

International Venture Handbooks

Applying for a United States Visa: A Practical Guide to the New Immigration Law Richard Fleischer

The Canadian Immigration Handbook: A Step-by-Step Guide to Processing Your Visa Application M J Bjarnason

Doing Business in Germany: A Practical Handbook for Business Owners and Managers Dan Finlay

Selling Into Japan: Essential Steps for Western Business Representatives Sadahiko Nakamura

Your Own Business in Europe: How to Branch Out or Start Up a New Business in Europe Mark Hempshell

Your Own Business in France: A Practical Guide to Setting Up an Independent Business or Profession in France Sam Crabb

Working Abroad: Essential Financial Planning for Expatriates & their Employers Jonathan Golding

Working in the Gulf: An Expatriate's Guide to Employment Law in the Gulf Arab States, Hamid Atiyyah

Your Own Business in Europe

How to Branch Out or Start Up a New Business in Europe

Mark Hempshell

International Venture Handbooks

Other books by the same author

Live and Work in France
How to Get a Job in Europe
How to Get a Job in France

British Library Cataloguing-in-Publication data

A catalogue record for this book is available from the British Library.

First published in 1994 by International Venture Handbooks,
a division of How To Books Ltd, Plymbridge House, Estover Road,
Plymouth PL6 7PZ, United Kingdom. Tel: Plymouth (0752)
695745/735251. Fax: (0752) 695699. Telex: 45635.

Note: The information in this book was accurate at the time of
writing. However, details are subject to continual change and readers
must confirm details for themselves before making further plans. In
particular, it is essential to take professional legal and financial advice
regarding particular proposed business. You are advised not to travel
to a particular country without first confirming the residence
regulations, business licensing, and business and financial law of that
country.

Typeset by Concept Typesetting Ltd, Salisbury.
Printed and bound in the United Kingdom by BPC Wheatons Ltd, Exeter.

Preface

As a country in which to start a business Britain has always offered good potential. The consumer economy developed successfully and matured in the late 1980s. Despite periods of lesser or greater recession a strong enterprise culture still prevails.

But, in the 1990s, there is a problem: In global terms the UK is a village, with 57 million local consumers at most; and that limits every business trading in Britain alone. Time and again, it is the inward-looking locally based businesses which fail; but in the global nineties it is those looking out to the wider world of opportunities that are succeeding and will grow. Are you ready to seize the new opportunites of business in Europe? As a place to set up in business continental Europe has even more going for it than Britain. The European Community (EC) has emerged as the largest trading unit in the world, with a massive consumer population of 340 million—and a grand total of 497 million in Europe as a whole.

The creation of the Single European Market (SEM) is an epochal event indeed. The countries of the EC are still independent sovereign states with their own laws, languages and customs. But now they are co-operating in many important areas so that many of the old barriers to trade—such as tariffs and quotas and different product standards—have gone. So far as doing business goes, if in no other way, Europe is a single country.

This Single Market is here and now. Whether the Maastricht Treaty on greater European union survives or fails the benefits and opportunities described in this book are already waiting to be exploited. The fact is, that if you are capable of running a viable business in Britain, you should be able to do the same thing in continental Europe.

In a continent of 497 million consumers there is an opening for everybody: big business, small business, professional practice, commercial, industrial, or retirement business. Whether you are looking to move to Europe, open a branch, or start up for the first time, prosperous European customers are waiting for you.

Although it is still early days for the Single European Market, this book sets out to unlock some of the many opportunities already available.

5

The philosophy behind this book is simple: why choose from just one country for your business when you can choose from 12 or more?

I gratefully acknowledge the help of the Commission of the European Communities (London and Brussels), DTI, North of England EuroInfo-Centre, Arthur Andersen, Touche Ross, Price Waterhouse, The Law Society, Lloyds Bank, Barclays Bank and the various EC Embassies who have greatly helped by providing up-to-date information on their services.

Mark Hempshell

Contents

Illustrations

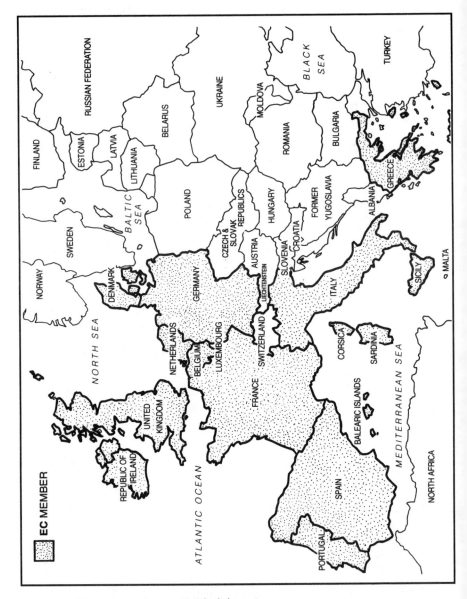

Fig. 1. The European Community (shaded areas).

1
Europe — Open for Business

A NEW WAY OF LOOKING AT BUSINESS

If someone today entrusted you with £250 000, a business plan, and sent you off to start a business, what would you do? Would you start with the first opportunity offered to you, and set up just round the corner? Hardly! Any reasonably intelligent person would want to research the situation carefully: find out where the best markets are; where the best land or property is; find a location with the best communications and sources of supply; find the cheapest or best trained labour—and all in relation to the product or service in question.

This is the freedom that is yours in Europe. No longer do you have to restrict your business to the UK. You can set up wherever in Europe you feel would be most suitable, whenever you like, and wherever you feel the best profits can be made.

There is now a general right to set up a business in any European Community (EC) country for citizens of any other EC country. Many of the practical barriers have been removed. Today, you are free to start or extend your business in any one of 12 European countries:

Belgium	Germany	Netherlands
Denmark	Greece	Portugal
Eire	Italy	Spain
France	Luxembourg	United Kingdom

The choice is even wider if you consider the non-EC European countries who do not grant the same automatic right but are certainly keener than ever to attract new investment. When starting a business no longer need you choose between Leeds or Liverpool—you can choose the best place for your business—from Leeds or Liverpool or Limoges or Liège or Livorno or Las Palmas or even, if you are so inclined, Łódź!

The key to the success of the European business in the 1990s is to choose your optimum location. The old idea of locating in a second-best place, simply because its laws and regulations were less onerous, is a dying one. The whole of Europe is very much open for business.

BASIC REQUIREMENTS FOR SETTING UP IN EUROPE

What you need

The idea of a business in Europe being only for existing firms is now largely outmoded. Anyone has the right, within the EC, and most of the practical barriers have been removed. Nevertheless, there are certain basic requirements:

1. *A business idea*

There are so many opportunities in Europe including for many businesses which scarcely exist in the UK.

2. *Capital*

In some countries any given capital injection will go further; in others it buys less. The cost and availability of finance may be more or less favourable elsewhere.

3. *A skill*

Those starting up in Europe should have some worthwhile skill to offer. Many trades and professions can now be carried out in the EC since many professional qualifications are now valid in every member state.

4. *Language knowledge*

The Single European Market has done little to remove language barriers. Ideally, you need a good basic knowledge of a European language in addition to English. Opportunities for setting up without language ability do exist but are more restricted.

At the end of the day, however, these tangible requirements are no more important than enthusiasm and commitment. You should feel comfortable with the country and the people. It pays to be in love with Tuscany or Andalucia or wherever. Setting up a business in a foreign country is always going to be more difficult than setting up at home. You must like problems and enjoy solving them!

You do NOT need:

Knowledge of local standards

In the EC many of these are now harmonised, although some time for settling in will be needed.

Local qualifications
Your UK trade and professional qualifications may well be acceptable in the EC.

Special consent
You have a legal right to set up anywhere in the EC, and to live there, and take your family. Any registration or licensing requirements are exactly the same as apply to nationals of that country.

Legal, accountancy or specialist business knowledge
If you lack this expertise it can be 'bought in' from professional advisers.

AM I SUITED TO DOING BUSINESS IN EUROPE?

Running a business abroad can make very good practical sense. It may be cheaper to start up than in the UK. It may be easier to start up than in the UK. There might be more money to be made. But it is easy to be too idealistic—many people dream of conducting business at a leisurely pace under sunny Mediterranean skies.

There are no accurate statistics to measure the success of expatriate businesses or branches of British businesses. But experts suggest that it is more risky than starting up at home. In Britain about one in three businesses fail in their first five years; in Europe this may be one in two. The European businessman or woman must be prepared to take extra risk, and allow greater contingency planning to deal with it.

By and large a European business is for those who would start in the UK, but want to take advantage of the greater challenges and wider range of opportunities. If you can suceed in the tough UK market you'll stand a good chance at succeeding in Europe. But a European business is not an alternative to the UK—if you don't think you could succeed in the UK, it is unlikely you would do so elsewhere in Europe.

Some people will elect to move lock, stock and barrel to Europe. Others will prefer to establish a branch of an existing UK business. Generally, starting a branch softens the risk but single-site businesses do benefit from personal supervision of an owner-operator.

Questions to ask yourself

- What money can I raise? Which country is the best to invest it in?

- What ideas and skills do I have? Which country is the best to utilise those in?

- Which European language do I have some knowledge of? If none, which would I feel happiest about learning?

- Am I prepared to put my capital at greater risk in the hope of a better return/way of life?

- What do my family think?

- Am I prepared to work twice as hard as for a UK business? (A conservative estimate!)

And, very importantly:

- Would my chosen business work better in the UK? If, for example, you want to start a fish and chip shop you might succeed with one in a Spanish tourist resort but it will always be easier in the UK. Don't go to Europe for Europe's sake!

Important principle
Start with your business proposition and find the right country to locate in. If you start with your preferred country and find a business to fit it is bound to be more difficult.

Pros and cons
Pros
- It is cheaper to set up in business in some European countries than in the UK; expenses are lower.

- Some countries have cheaper land and property.

- Some countries have cheaper/more readily available finance.

- Government incentives may be available in some places.

- Many countries have larger and/or less developed consumer and industrial markets.

- Wages and profits may be higher. For example, German executives may earn (and spend) twice as much as their British colleagues.

- Some countries have a pleasant pace of life—the French pavement café or Spanish bar is a popular dream.

Cons
- Some countries have much greater setting up costs. Property is expensive to buy.

- Most countries have more complex bureaucracy than in the UK, in spite of the Single European Market.

- Business profits may be lower; in some countries the smallest enterprises only offer subsistence living.

- Life in some countries is hectic and chaotic—business lurches along in a disorganised fashion.

- In some places it may be hard to get suitable stock, reliable equipment and properly trained staff.

- Locals may resent foreign business people, especially if they are successful.

- The language barrier still exists and is more of a problem in business.

Important principle
The disadvantages, even in a 'safe bet-least risk' situation are always going to be very major. You must be fairly sure that the advantages are more than going to make up for this. For most people, this means: at the end of the day are we going to make more money—and have a more interesting and rewarding business and social life?

SOME CASE HISTORIES

Example 1: David Ward and Michelle Palmer
UK location
Rotherham, South Yorks.

Business proposition
Purchase and run a small bar in Benidorm, Spain.

Capital available
£12 000 from sale of house (sale price £33 000 less £21 000 mortgage), plus £5 000 savings.

Result
Purchased freehold of bar in Benidorm for 2 810 000 Ptas (approximately £16 000) plus stock. Rent small flat nearby.

Comments
In summer both work 10am–4am, 6 days a week. Net profits in first year were 1 196 500 Ptas (approx. £6 800).

Personal Action Plan

Action	Further reference in this book
1. Consider what sort of business you could and would like to set up.	Chapter 3
2. Estimate a ball park figure for available capital—sale of existing property or business, cash value of investments, possible finance etc.	Chapter 4
3. Consider what country would be the best base for your business.	Chapter 8
4. Investigate potential in chosen country. Is there a good demand for your products or services?	Chapter 3
5. Investigate any licensing and qualification considerations. Are your trade/professional qualifications transferable?	Chapter 2
6. Consider legal position, structure of business most suitable in that country.	Chapter 5
7. Investigate practical considerations— property, personnel etc.	Chapter 6
8. Consider how you feel about living in the country in question.	Chapter 7
9. Start to make preliminary arrangements to start the business.	
10. If plans falter, return to first step and consider another country.	

Fig. 2. A personal action plan for doing business in Europe

Example 2: Gordon and Eve Ellison
UK location Leicester

Business proposition
To live and work in Italy, preferably Tuscany. Eve to continue her business as a designer (serving clients in the UK). Gordon to take semi-retirement, perhaps with small sideline businesses.

Capital available
£185 000 cash from the sale of their house, plus £55 000 savings. Also pension income.

Result
Bought house and land near Volterra for £190 000. Converted farm buildings in the grounds for resale. Rented land to a local farmer.

Comments
At the time of writing Gordon wishes to launch a summer school in an unoccupied part of the house teaching English and painting, but is experiencing problems with the local bureaucracy—'. . . plans would probably not be viable were it not for our existing sources of income'.

Example 3: Michael Forth
UK location London SW15.

Business proposition
As partner in a London property consultancy wished to set up in France to take advantage of British interest in holiday property, and lessen the impact of the UK recession on his business at home.

Capital available
Access to commercial finance package of up to £85 000.

Result
Targeted Montreuil in Pas-de-Calais département as a likely place to start business but due to local bureaucracy and lack of local knowledge found it impractical to set up on his own. After some negotiation set up in partnership with a local French estate agent, injecting 500 000 FF into a new company. Now handles UK end of operation, marketing properties supplied by the French partner.

Comments
Spends about 10 days every month in France and has bought a house near Hesdin as a pied-à-terre.

2
Residence, Licences and Qualifications in Europe

WHAT THE SINGLE EUROPEAN MARKET MEANS

The Single European Market (SEM) was established by the Single European Act (SEA). This document was adopted by all the EC members in 1986 and came into force in 1987 with a target date of 1 January 1993 for the implementation of all its aims.

Although tariffs and quotas between EC members were dissolved as far back as 1 July 1968 it became clear in the late 1970s and early 1980s that the EC was still not a common market as proposed in the 1957 Treaty of Rome. Numerous non-tariff barriers, such as customs checks, border controls, differing product standards and differing professional qualifications were still hampering trade between members.

The SEA sets out to remove these non tariff barriers by a wide range of measures completed on 1 January 1993. There are four overall aims of the Single European Market:

Aim	Example of measures taken
Free movement of goods	Removal of customs and border controls. Harmonisation of product standards
Free movement of services	Rights for businesses from one member to operate in another. Harmonisation of some standards.
Free movement of capital	Removal of exchange controls. Changes to banking system.
Free movement of people	Right to work in other member states. Harmonisation of many qualifications.

The main aim of the SEM is, largely, that doing business with another EC country should not be hampered by any barriers which do not apply to your competitors in that other member state. So, the right to establish business in another country is not strictly an objective of the SEM, but an essential consequence if it is to work properly.

Apart from the general right to establish business the entrepreneur is aided by the fact that many standards, regulations and some laws are now 'harmonised' (the accepted EC term for making a standard the same or similar throughout different member states). However, it is not that simple: Member countries can and do still impose different regulations and standards on businesses in their country and these must be followed by foreign business people. The only important proviso is that these must not discriminate against foreign business people.

At the time of writing it is likely that many of the measures of the SEM may take several years to take effect, so problems and discrepancies in taking advantage of harmonisation and other changes must be expected and allowed for.

The Single European Market is expected to result in a minimum 5% increase in Gross National Product of the EC member states as a whole.

YOUR RIGHT TO SET UP IN EUROPE

In order that the Single Market be truly effective there is now a right for any citizen of any EC member state to establish a business or exercise their profession in any of the other member states. Local law or different local standards in qualifications cannot be used to exclude non-nationals from business in other EC countries.

However, this does not mean that EC citizens have totally free access to start a business. EC countries are entitled to impose their own registration and control procedures on those operating a business, exactly as happens in the UK. All of them do and all of these systems are more complicated than those in the UK. The main benefit is that they must treat nationals and other EC citizens alike.

Most other EC countries demand that those starting a trade or profession are experienced and qualified accordingly. This is demanded for many more businesses than in the UK. The main benefit is that they must usually accept your UK experience and qualifications.

Non EC countries

Non EC countries are perfectly entitled to exclude non nationals if they wish and impose whatever regulations regarding qualifications, finance and so on that they wish. However, most welcome anyone planning to make a business investment.

The European Community

FACT FILE

The European Community (EC) was founded in 1957 with the sign-
ing of the Treaty of Rome. The UK joined in 1973. The 12 members
are now France, Germany, Belgium, Netherlands, Luxembourg,
Denmark, Italy, Greece, Spain, Portugal, Eire and the United Kingdom. Other nations are likely to join in the future.

- The EC is not regarded as a single country. All 12 members are
  still independent sovereign states.

- The EC does not share a universal economic system.

- The EC does not share a universal system of government or
  politics.

- The EC does not have a universal law. Laws in every EC country
  are the responsibility of each individual Government.

- But the EC *can* create laws and force members to adopt them.

- The EC countries do now have universal standards for many
  things, such as product standards, qualifications etc.

- The EC countries do not share tastes, customs and language.

- Nationals of one EC country have a right to live, work and
  establish business in any other EC country.

- Nationals of one EC country living in another are resident aliens, not citizens of that country. They DO NOT share all the
  rights and obligations of nationals.

Fig. 3. The European Community fact file.

RESIDENCE REQUIREMENTS

Residence for business purposes in EC countries

EC citizens wishing to set up business in another EC country do not need visas or work permits. It is possible to travel to any of these countries and live there with a view to starting a business without any prior consent.

You will need a residence permit if you wish to live in that country, rather than just do business or establish a branch there. The procedures for this are the same as for those who are working. It is advisable to start the application for a residence permit immediately after arrival, although you can remain in each country for 90 days without a residence permit.

The Embassy or Consulate of the respective country will advise you of the procedure. Permits are usually issued at the town hall of the town or city where you intend to live. In some cases the main police station handles this instead. You will need:

- an application form
- your passport
- passport photographs (often up to six).

Requirements vary from country to country and office to office and some will also require such documents as:

- evidence of business or self-employment, such as a copy of your entry on the Commercial Register, or a membership of the local Chamber of Commerce
- evidence of means (a bank statement from a local bank or cash: the amount varies from country to country)
- deeds showing property purchased, or a lease
- birth and marriage certificates
- a health clearance certificate from a local hospital.

As a result it pays to be prepared before leaving the UK. Even within the EC there are no uniform requirements and although you may be entitled to a residence permit each country can apply its own procedure.

Dependants of those obtaining residence permits for the purpose of running a business are usually granted automatic residence too, but must still apply for a permit.

Residence for business purposes in non EC countries

No non EC country in Europe offers any special concessions to non nationals wishing to establish a business in their country. Most will consider those wishing to do this, but usually on the basis that they are making a capital investment. There may be a minimum sum of investment or finance without which you will not be granted permission.

If actually intending to take up residence, rather than open a branch, you will need a business immigration visa or similar. You may also need a work permit to work in the business and a residence permit. Both must normally be applied for before moving to the country.

As applications for consents of this nature are few each tends to be treated on its merits. The Embassy or Consulate of the respective country will provide fuller details. Usually you will have to make out a case for your visa. The following information may be required:

- a business plan
- details of capital available and finance
- details of locals to be employed, now and in the future
- details of professional advisers retained.

BUSINESS REGISTRATION, INCORPORATION AND LICENSING

Registration

The regulations which apply to business registration vary from country to country. Even the EC countries may set their own regulations and dictate the procedure for registering.

In most countries it is necessary for every business to be registered with a Government agency, usually known as the Commercial Registry or Trade Registry. This usually applies to unincorporated organisations such as sole traders as well as to incorporated companies. You cannot set up a business without registering, as sole traders or partnerships do all the time in the UK.

Registration is often a formality but you may need to supply:

- a certificate of incorporation, if appropriate

- your own residence permit

- evidence of means

- evidence of registration with the local income tax/VAT/social security/environmental health authorities

- evidence of registration with a trade or professional body where local law requires those operating this trade or profession to be so registered, eg doctors or accountants

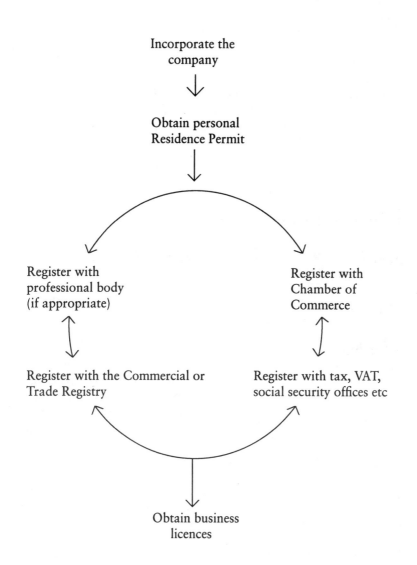

Fig. 4. The business registration roundabout. The procedure for registering, incorporating and licensing a business varies in every country and is frequently a Catch-22 situation, but the best procedure is often as shown above.

- professional qualifications, where appropriate

- evidence of experience in this trade. Some countries require this. Usually, evidence that you have operated the business in the UK or been employed in such a business will suffice.

In some countries businesses must also register with the local Chamber of Commerce before the official registration will be accepted. To do this it is usually necessary to produce the evidence required in the last three steps above.

Incorporation

Information about incorporating a company in Europe, ie creating a legal business entity such as a private limited company, will be found in Chapter 5 and Chapter 8.

In most countries the formation of an incorporated company must be handled by a lawyer and the documents forming the company must be endorsed by a notary public, both of whom may receive a commission based on the paid up share capital of the company.

Incorporated companies must usually still be registered with the Commercial Registry as well as a Registrar of Companies.

Licensing

The regulations on business licensing are subject to different national laws, even in other EC countries. As a result certain types of trade require licensing in some countries but not in others. Some harmonisation has taken place in order to remove barriers to trade, but there are no plans to standardise licensing totally across the EC. So, for example, the regulations relating to food hygiene are similar across the EC but the way they are interpreted and implemented varies from country to country—in Germany the authorities are strict, in Greece they may be more lenient.

Licensing cannot be used to keep out a product which is in free circulation in another EC country. So, for example, new British made cars cannot be kept out of the French market by the imposition of different safety standards.

In general, businesses which tend to require licensing are those involved with:

- catering and food handling
- sale of alcohol
- handling drugs, poisons, chemicals and fuels
- medical or health products/services
- operation of motor vehicles

- financial advice or brokerage
- any business involving pollution, health or safety risks
- in some countries, any manufacturing business
- in many European countries, hairdressers require licences.

The extent of licensing in your preferred country should be investigated at an early stage. The appropriate Embassy or Consulate should be able to pass on contact addresses. Advice can also be offered by:

BSI Enquiry Services. Tel: (0908) 221166.
Technical Help to Exporters (THE). Tel: (0908) 220022.

Both are based at Linford Wood, Milton Keynes, Bucks MK14 6LE.

YOUR BUSINESS QUALIFICATIONS AND EXPERIENCE

Using your qualifications in Europe
One way of setting up business in Europe is for those with trade or professional qualifications to conduct their current trade or profession there. This is now permitted on the basis that many UK trade and professional qualifications are now acceptable in any EC country.

There are 2 systems under which this is possible:

Harmonised Training Directives
Here, the training courses across the EC for selected qualifications are deemed to offer largely the same programme of training. This applies to doctors, dentists, nurses, midwives, vets, architects, pharmacists, GPs and those in road transport.

The First General System of Mutual Recognition of Qualifications
Here, the training courses may be different but the qualification is of a similar standard. This applies to all qualifications obtained after three years post secondary study, plus all lesser qualifications in certain fields which currently are: manufacturing/processing industries, food/beverage industries, wholesale trades, intermediaries in commerce and industry, retail trade, wholesale coal trade, trade in toxic products, hotel/catering, insurance agents/brokers, transport/travel agency, hairdressing, some fishery, postal and telecommunications, recreational, community and personal services. More sectors are to be added, together with recognition for school qualifications.

Under EC directives those qualified to work in one profession in one EC state are usually qualified to undertake it in another. This does not remove the need to be aware of differing local situations and, ideally, to speak the local language. The basis on which this operates is usually that your qualification will entitle you to join the appropriate professional body which governs your trade or profession in the respective country. This, in turn, entitles you to register or licence your business under the appropriate national laws, as discussed earlier.

In some cases professionals wishing to operate in another EC country may have to undergo an examination, or complete a period of supervised work, before they will be accepted.

The requirement of 'experience'

In some cases it will be found that qualifications or experience are required to operate a specific trade or profession in the EC, whereas they are *not* in the UK. This does not, however, mean that British citizens who are competent, but not qualified, in that trade or profession are barred from operating it in the EC.

The **European Community Certificate of Experience** exists so that your experience can be recognised and used to operate a trade or profession legally in an EC country. Certificates are issued by the Department of Trade & Industry (DTI) in the UK who will look at your experience (which you should be able to prove), look at the relevant EC directives, and decide if you qualify for a certificate.

The trades and professions for which a Certificate of Experience is required varies from country to country. The experience required to be granted one which will be accepted in most EC countries is usually:

- Six years experience of running your own business, or managing a business, in the field in question, in the UK. Or:

- Three years experience as above, plus three years previous training in that activity.

- Three years experience of running your own business, plus five years of non-management employment in that field.

- Five years experience in that field, preceded by three years training for a relevant national qualification.

Example
Jason Black has run his own hairdressing business in his home town for seven years and, although being unqualified, which is perfectly legal in the UK, has established a good reputation. Having holidayed in France for many years and become competent in spoken French he decides to set up in business in Lyon.

Jason finds out that hairdressers in France must have a professional qualification to operate legally. So he applies to the DTI for a Certificate of Experience. The DTI examine the relevant EC directive (82/489) and decide that he qualifies for a Certificate of Experience.

On arrival in France Jason goes to the local Chambre des Métiers who examine his certificate and his experience and decide that, under their own rules, he qualifies for membership. The Chambre also helps him apply for a Carte de Qualification Professionnelle de Coiffeur from the local Préfecture.

Membership of the Chambre and possession of the Carte permits Jason to trade legally as a self employed hairdresser in France, even though he does not have a French qualification.

NON EC COUNTRIES

UK qualifications and experience are not usually officially recognised in non EC countries, although they may be respected. In such cases it is worth checking with the appropriate foreign professional body as it may be possible for your qualifications to be officially recognised, perhaps following an examination, or a period of supervised practice or training.

DOCUMENTATION PROCEDURES

Even where UK qualifications are considered equivalent to those in European countries it is usually necessary to have them officially recognised in the respective country if intending to be self-employed (though often not if becoming an employee). Applications for recognition must usually be made to a professional association or a chamber of commerce. Specimen application forms appear at the end of this chapter.

Finding out more

Further information on residence regulations is available from the respective Embassy or Consulate. Further information on licensing and qualifications is available from:

● DTI, 123 Victoria Street, London SW1E 6RB. Tel: (071) 215 5000.

● Employment Department, Qualifications and Standards Branch, Room E603, Moorfoot, Sheffield S1 4PQ. Tel: (0742) 594144.

● Your UK trade or professional body.

- The appropriate foreign trade or professional body. Ask your UK trade or professional body for an address or referral.

- Commission of the European Communities, 8 Storey's Gate, London SW1P 3AT. Tel: (071) 973 1992.

- The Employment Service—Explanatory leaflet CVQE1 *Comparability of Vocational Qualifications in the EEC.*

- Specific information about business licensing and registration can be found in the *Guide to the Establishment of Enterprises and Craft Businesses in the European Community,* published by the Commission of the European Communities. This and other EC publications are available from HMSO Books, HMSO Publications Centre, 51 Nine Elms Lane, London SW8 5DR. Tel: (071) 873 9090.

HOW TO MASTER LANGUAGES
Roger Jones

With the expansion of international travel and the advent of the global market, languages are more valuable than ever before. Written for business people, students and others, this book discusses: why learn a language, which language to choose, language training and where to find it, getting down to language learning, children and languages, and language training in organisations. A huge reference section completes the book, giving information on an enormous variety of courses, guides and study material, providing an overview of the world's myriad languages and their use today. Roger Jones DipTESL is himself an experienced linguist, writer and educational consultant.

£8.99, 160pp illus. 1 85703 0923

Please add postage & packing (UK 1.00 per copy. Europe £2.00 per copy World £3.00 per copy airmail).
How To Books Ltd, Plymbridge House, Estover Road, Plymouth PL6 7PZ, United Kingdom. Tel: (0752) 695745. Fax: (0752) 695699. Telex: 45635.

Credit card orders may be faxed or phoned.

Absender:

Antrag nebst Anlagen
in zweifacher Ausfertigung erbeten

Antrag auf Erteilung einer Ausnahmebewilligung gemäß § 8 oder § 9
des Gesetzes zur Ordnung des Handwerks (HwO) zur selbständigen
Ausübung des _____-Handwerks

1. _____
2. unbeschränkt
3. beschränkt auf folgende wesentliche Tätigkeiten
   (genau bezeichnen!) _____ 1)
4. befristet bis zum . .19 (s.Ziffer. 11 des Fragebogens) _____
   unbefristet

5. Name, Vorname   geborene(r)   geboren am
   Geburtsort   Staatsangehörigkeit   PLZ/Wohnort
   Straße   Telefon mit Vorwahl

6. Ich beabsichtige am . .19
   □ die Neuerrichtung eines Betriebes
   □ den Eintritt als Betriebsleiter in den Betrieb
   □ eine Betriebsübernahme von
   □ den Eintritt als Mitinhaber in den Betrieb
   □ die Erweiterung eines Betriebes

   Genaue Bezeichnung des Unternehmens
   PLZ/Betriebsort   Straße   Telefon mit Vorwahl

7. Neben dem Handwerk, für das die Ausnahmebewilligung beantragt
   wird, soll noch folgendes Gewerbe betrieben werden (genaue
   Bezeichnung, z.B. Einzelhandel):
   mit _____, anderes Handwerk _____ ,
   handwerksähnliches Gewerbe _____ .

8. Berufsausbildung und bisherige berufliche Tätigkeit:
   a) Abschluß- oder Abgangszeugnis der Schule (genaue Bezeichnung, Ort) 2)
   b) Lehrzeit als
      vom . .19 bis . .19
   c) Gesellenprüfung/Facharbeiterprüfung abgelegt am . .19
      vor 2)
   d) Sonstige Lehrgänge und Prüfungen (z.B. Werkmeister, Indu-
      striemeister, Techniker, Handwerksmeister, Abschlußprüfung
      an Hochschule oder Fachhochschule, Fachkurse und Lehrgänge):2)

Fig. 5. Typical form used in Germany to apply to the local Chamber of Crafts/Chamber of Trade for a foreign tradesman to set up as a self-employed tradesman.

e) Lückenlose Aufzählung der beruflichen Tätigkeiten seit Beendigung der Ausbildung als Arbeitnehmer oder Selbständiger einschließlich Bundeswehr, bis zur Antragstellung 1)

von	bis	Tätigkeit (genaue Bezeichnung) Arbeitgeber mit Adresse (soweit möglich)

9. Stehen Sie z.Z. in einem Arbeitsverhältnis
   ☐ ja, als
   ☐ nein, arbeitslos seit dem . .19
   gemeldet beim Arbeitsamt in
   Grund für die Arbeitslosigkeit
   ☐ Ich bin selbständig als

10. Hatten Sie bereits eine Ausnahmebewilligung?

Ausstellungsbehörde	Datum	Aktenzeichen

11. Angaben zur Meisterprüfung:
    Sind Sie bereit, die Meisterprüfung in dem Handwerk, für das die Ausnahmebewilligung beantragt wird, abzulegen?
    ☐ ja
    ☐ nein
    Zur Vorbereitung auf die Meisterprüfung habe ich besucht, besuche ich oder werde ich besuchen:
    Fachkursus vom . .19 bis . .19
    bei

Allgemeintheoretischer und berufspädagogischer Kursus
vom . .19 bis . .19
bei
Die Gebühr(en) für diese(n) Kurs(e) habe ich bereits bezahlt 2)
☐ ja
☐ nein
Zur Ablegung der Meisterprüfung habe ich mich bereits am . .19 bei der Handwerkskammer in angemeldet.
Folgende Teilprüfungen sind bereits mit Erfolg abgelegt:

Die Meisterprüfung wird voraussichtlich vollständig abgelegt sein am . .19 .

12. Waren Sie bereits in der Handwerksrolle eingetragen?
    ☐ nein
    ☐ ja, und zwar bei der Handwerkskammer in

13. Nur für Antragsteller, die in einem anderen EWG-Land im Handwerk gearbeitet haben:
    a) abgeschlossene Lehre
       ☐ ja
       ☐ nein

Handwerk	von	bis	2)

    b) Tätigkeit als Unselbständiger im -Handwerk
       vom . .19 bis . .19
    c) Tätigkeit als Selbständiger oder Betriebsleiter
       vom . .19 bis . .19 3)
       bei (genaue Bezeichnung des Betriebes oder der Betriebe)

14. Nach meiner bisherigen Ausbildung und Tätigkeit qualifizieren mich folgende Fachkenntnisse und Fertigkeiten zum selbständigen Betreiben des Handwerks, für welches ich die Ausnahmebewilligung beantrage:

Fig. 5. continued

15.   Begründung des Ausnahmeantrages

Hier sind die Gründe ausführlich zu erläutern, weshalb Sie mit der Ausübung
des selbständigen Handwerks nicht warten können, bis Sie die Meisterprüfung
abgelegt haben oder weshalb die Ablegung der Meisterprüfung für Sie eine un-
zumutbare Belastung ist. Außerdem ist anzugeben, weshalb die Meisterprüfung
nicht in den zurückliegenden Jahren abgelegt wurde. 1)

16.   Wollen Sie eine Berufsvereinigung, z.B. Innung, benennen, die zu
      Ihrem Antrag gehört werden soll? Falls ja, welche?

17.   ☐ Ich bin bereit,

      ☐ Ich bin nicht bereit,

      auf eventuelle Anordnung des Regierungspräsidenten die notwen-
      digen Kenntnisse und Fertigkeiten in einer Überprüfung vor
      einem Sachverständigen auf meine Kosten unter Beweis zu stel-
      len.

18.   Ich versichere, daß meine vorstehenden Angaben vollständig sind
      und der Wahrheit entsprechen.

      Mir ist bekannt, daß die Entscheidung gebührenpflichtig ist
      und daß ich das Handwerk erst ausüben darf, wenn ich in der
      Handwerksrolle eingetragen bin.

      _____ , den .   .19

      _____
      (Unterschrift des Antragstellers

                                        Antrag zweifach einreichen:

                                        Für den Regierungspräsidenten
                                        für die Handwerkskammer

Fig. 5. continued

Model C   Dossier no.

AANVRAAGFORMULIER TER VERKRIJGING VAN EEN ONTHEFFING OP GROND VAN
DE VESTIGINGSWET BEDRIJVEN 1954, ARTIKEL 15, EERSTE LID

Ingediend bij

1. Ondernemer(s):	I	II	III
a. naam en voornamen			
b. adres			
c. geboorteplaats en -datum			
d. telefoon			

2. Bedrijfsleider:	
A. a. naam en voornamen	
b. adres	
c. geboorteplaats en -datum	

3. Beheerder:	
A. a. naam en voornamen	
b. adres	
c. geboorteplaats en -datum	

4. Rechtsvorm:	Handelsnaam:

5. Adres v. d. $\frac{\text{Inrichting}}{\text{Onderneming}}$ Gemeente: Plaats:

Adres:

6. Bedrijfsomschrijving:

a. voor de uitoefening van welk(e) bedrijf(ven) wordt ontheffing aangevraagd (de branche(s) aanduiden)

b. heeft deze aanvraag betrekking op de uitoefening van het bedrijf in volledige of nagenoeg volledige omvang?   Ja/Neen

c. indien de bedrijfsuitvoering niet volledig zal zijn, welke bedrijfshandelingen zullen dan worden verricht?

7. Welke diploma's of verklaringen legt u hierbij over met betrekking tot:

a. de bedrijfsleider:

b. de beheerder:

Fig. 6. Example of a form used in the Netherlands to apply to the Chamber of Commerce and Industry for foreign trade and professional qualifications to be recognised. (A European Community Certificate of Experience may also need to be supplied.)

8. *a.* Welk(e) bedrijf (bedrijven) wordt (worden) als een hoofdbestanddeel uitgeoefend van de bedrijfsuitoefening in de betrokken onderneming of inrichting?

b. Is voor de uitoefening van dit bedrijf (bedrijven) vergunning of ontheffing ingevolge de Vestigingswet Bedrijven 1954 verleend en zo ja, wanneer?

9. Waarom vraagt U ontheffing aan? (Zo volledig mogelijk motiveren).
(Bijzondere omstandigheden en opleiding alsmede ervaring zo volledig mogelijk beschrijven; eventuele bewijsstukken overleggen).

Ondergetekende verklaart hiermede, dat de bovenstaande, c.q. de in de bijlage(n) vermelde toelichting een juiste en volledige weergave bevat van alle feiten en omstandigheden welke door hem aan de Kamer van Koophandel ter kennis zijn gebracht teneinde voor de gevraagde ontheffing in aanmerking te komen.

te

de   19

Aldus naar waarheid ingevuld
De aanvrager(s)

Aanvrager(s) wordt erop gewezen, dat een onjuiste of onvolledige beantwoording van de gestelde vragen kan leiden tot weigering of intrekking van de ontheffing en strafbaar is.

NIET DOOR AANVRAGER IN TE VULLEN

Kredietwaardigheid

De ondernemer(s) voldoet (voldoen) wel / niet aan de gestelde eisen van kredietwaardigheid.

Datum binnenkomst:	Beslissing nemen voor:	Betaald leges /
Vestigingsbesluit(en):		Artikel(en):

ADVIES:

Fig. 6. continued

ΠΡΟΣ:

Α Ι Τ Η Σ Η

ΤΟ ΒΙΟΤΕΧΝΙΚΟ ΕΠΙΜΕΛΗΤΗΡΙΟ ΑΘΗΝΑΣ
ΤΜΗΜΑ ΜΗΤΡΩΟΥ
Ε Ν Τ Α Υ Θ Α

Για τη χορήγηση πιστοποιητικού στα
Μητρώα του Βιοτεχνικού Επιμελητηρίου
Αθήνας.
ΣΤΟΙΧΕΙΑ ΑΙΤΟΥΣΑΣ ΕΠΙΣΕΙΡΗΣΗΣ:

Σας παρακαλούμε να μας χορηγή-
σετε πιστοποιητικό εγγραφής της επι-
χείρησής μας,στα διατηρούμενα μητρώα

ΕΠΩΝΥΜΙΑ.......................
....
....

του Επιμελητηρίου να το χρησιμοποιή-
σουμε για.......................
....

ΑΝΤΙΚΕΙΜΕΝΟ ΔΡΑΣΤΗΡΙΟΤΗΤΑΣ:
....
....

....
....

ΔΙΕΥΘΥΝΣΗ:
....
....

Ο ΑΙΤΩΝ

ΣΥΝΟΙΚΙΑ:......................

ΤΗΚ:...........................

(ΣΦΡΑΓΙΣ ΕΠΙΧΕΙΡΗΣΗΣ)

ΑΡΙΘΜ.ΜΗΤΡΩΟΥ:..................
ΑΡΙΘΜ.ΔΕΛΤΙΟΘΗΚΗΣ:..............

Αθήνα.............

(Για τη χορήγηση πιστοποιητικού εγγραφής
απαιτούνται δύο χαρτόσημα των 20 δρχ.
Το ένα επικολλάται επί της αίτησηςκαι
το άλλο επί του πιστοποιητικού).

Fig. 7. Example of a form required in Greece to register a business and join the Chamber of Commerce.

3

Which Business to Set Up in Europe

YOUR BEST STRATEGY

Selection of the right business idea is paramount to any successful venture into Europe. It is especially important to set up in something you feel suited for and in which you feel confident. The golden rule is don't start something in Europe which you wouldn't feel happy about starting at home.

Overall, however, choice of the right country for you is probably the most important factor, and this will be considered later. If you choose the right country problems and difficulties are much easier to overcome. If you like France, for example, and can speak and write some French, then a business there is bound to be less fraught than one in Spain, even if you know you could buy a business much more cheaply in Spain.

Secondly, it is wise to select or reject each proposition on its merits. Technical details and problems can then be dealt with later. To have a business location unfettered by petty barriers is one of the most valuable spin-offs of the Single European Market.

It is still not easy to get reliable information on business propositions in Europe. It may be wise to begin a search for ideas some 12 or 18 months before your projected start-up date. During that time maintain and build a 'running list' of possibilities from which you can shortlist serious propositions.

Three sources of business propositions

1. Your current occupation

Your current occupation (or business) should be considered first as the object for a European business or branch. Current experience in a particular field counts for a great deal and may be more sought after in other countries.

2. Previous occupations

It is always worth reviewing all your past occupations to see how the skills which you have acquired could form the basis of a new business, perhaps with some updating. These skills might be more appropriate or sought after than the ones you use in your current occupation.

Make a list of any previous occupations and then evaluate them according to their current value. For example:

1978–82	Qualified plumber
1982–85	Heating engineer
1986–89	Sales executive, air conditioning
1990–present day	Sales manager, insurance industry

On this information, for example, you might decide to look at setting up a plumbing contracting business—on the basis that you wished to move to Spain and would find it easier to provide a technical service rather than work in sales and marketing which requires greater local language knowledge.

3. Supplementary training
There may be situations where you would consider retraining to widen your business options in Europe, and would do this before leaving the UK. You could do this by taking some academic or professional course, or by taking some job in the UK first. This experience could then be used to start a business in Europe.

Suppose, for example, that you wish to open a pavement café in France. In that country catering is very much considered a profession, rather than a business. If you were committed to start, but had no experience, it would be easier to get this in the UK first rather than France.

SOURCES OF IDEAS, INFORMATION AND ADVICE

Newspapers and business magazines
Check the main business newspapers and business magazines of Europe to keep yourself up-to-date on the latest business ideas, trends, and growth areas. It may be worth inspecting such periodicals regularly at main libraries, assuming you have some language knowledge. The most influential business magazines include:

Le Nouvel Economiste (France)
L' Expansion (France)
Der Spiegel (Germany)

Details of other publications can be found in *Benn's Media Directory Europe*.

UK newspapers also provide a background to European business ideas and trends. Useful newpapers to check include:

The Guardian
The Independent
The European

Using the high street banks

Apart from their services in finance and transmission of funds, the UK high street banks can also be a good source of information and advice on European countries and the Single Market. They can also arrange introductions to their branches or partner banks in Europe. Some can put you in touch with business advisers or potential partners in your chosen area.

NatWest
National Westminster Bank has developed a PC software package called PHAROS, which provides a comprehensive picture of how the Single Market affects existing businesses. Details are available from: National Westminster Bank, Freepost, London EC3B 3JL. Tel: (0800) 777888.

Barclays
Barclays Bank has a Trade Development Service which can help you research foreign markets and find suitable trading partners abroad.

Some services are charged for; other are free or free to customers only.

Contacts
Barclays	Your local Barclays Business Centre
Lloyds	Any high street branch
Midland	Freephone (0800) 289359
National Westminster	European Business Section (071) 375 6071

Using the embassies and consulates

Some foreign Embassies and Consulates are charged with the responsibility of attracting foreign investment; other do not consider this one of their functions. Those that are helpful can sometimes provide quite detailed information on:

● grants, incentives and loans
● contracts for local enterprise agencies in Europe
● lists of useful books, journals and directories

- introductions to government departments, Chambers of Commerce and business people
- lists of further contacts

British Embassies and Consulates in European countries are better equipped to help those wishing to export to their respective country, rather than those setting up in business. An enquiry by letter, 'phone or in person may produce useful leads.

Industrial Development Associations

Some European countries have national IDAs (Industrial Development Associations) whose function is to attract foreign investment to their country. For example, France has an organisation called DATAR (Délégation à l'Aménagement du Territoire et à l'Action Régionale), with an office in London.

IDAs can offer practical and financial help, and introduce many other contacts. Often, they are better geared up to helping those making a larger investment. The relevant Embassy can usually help if you have difficulty finding them.

Contacting local authorities

- in Europe
- in the UK

Local authorities in Europe are usually keen to attract foreign investment in their area, especially investment leading to new jobs. Consider approaching the local authorities—town, city, region or autonomous government—in your chosen region. Most have a specialist Economic Development Office (EDO). For example, every area of Germany has an Amt für Wirtschaftsförderung, or Ministerium für Wirtschaft, dealing with economic and industrial development.

You can obtain the addresses from Embassies, telephone directories for the area you are interested in (telephone directories for most European countries are at main libraries in the UK) or from the *European Municipal Directory* (European Directories Ltd).

Your own UK local authority may have a European Liaison Office which can advise.

Approaching the Chambers of Commerce

Chambers of Commerce vary in their enthusiasm but most are keen to promote international business links. Many can offer quite detailed advice and information on investment and business opportunities, and personal introductions to business partners in Europe. At the very least they should be able to suggest further contacts.

There are four types of Chambers of Commerce to consult:

- Your local Chamber of Commerce. See telephone directory if not already a member.

- The national Chamber of Commerce in the UK for the respective country. See addresses in Chapter 8.

- The British Chamber of Commerce in the respective country. Addresses in Chapter 8.

- Local Chambers of Commerce in European towns and cities. Ask the foreign Embassy for a referral or check the European telephone directories.

Information and contacts for UK and international Chambers of Commerce can also be obtained from the Association of British Chambers of Commerce, 9 Tufton Street, London SW1. Tel: (071) 222 1555. The Association of Chambers of Commerce and Industry in Europe (called Euro-Chambres) can be contacted at the same address.

Using trade and professional associations

UK trade and professional associations increasingly have links with their counterparts in European countries. These associations can be approached with a view to contacting European members and exchanging information on business propositions. At the very least they should be able to advise you on the status of any qualifications you hold (see Chapter 2).

Details of UK trade and professional associations can be found in *Trade Associations and Professional Bodies of the UK*, available at main libraries.

Details of trade and professional associations across Europe can be found in the *Directory of European Community Trade and Professional Associations* (Editions Delta).

Using the Department of Trade and Industry (DTI)

The overriding aim of the DTI is to help British businesses take full advantage of trading opportunities with Europe.

However, many of their services will be of interest not just to exporters, but to those wishing actually to set up in Europe. There are three services which are of particular interest:

DTI Exports to Europe Branch (EEB)
This service has a specialist bureau to advise on trading links with each
EC country:

Belgium and Luxembourg	(071) 215 5486
Denmark	(071) 215 4397
France	(071) 215 4762
Germany	(071) 215 4796
Greece	(071) 215 5103
Italy	(071) 215 5103
Netherlands	(071) 215 4790
Portugal	(071) 215 5103
Spain	(071) 215 5624
Multi-country enquiries	(071) 215 5336

Written enquiries can be made to: Exports to Europe Branch, DTI, Bay
956, Kingsgate House, 66–74 Victoria Street, London SW1E 6SW.

Your Local DTI Office
Can assist with general enquiries. Contact details appear at the end of the
book.

Export Market Information Centre (EMIC)
EMIC is an up-to-date library of overseas market intelligence which can
be used by all members of the public. It is particularly useful for statistics
and market research reports and is located at:

Ashdown House, 123 Victoria Street, London SW1E 6RB. Tel: (071)
215 5444. Opening hours Mon–Fri 9.30am–5.30pm.

The new European Information Centres (EICs)

The EICs, also known as EuroInfoCentres, are a network of 200 bureaux
across Europe, set up by the European Commission. They help companies by providing them with information on the European Community
and doing business in Europe. Their knowledge covers areas such as
product standards and EC grants and loans, amongst many other things.
EICs also have access to a wide network of contacts so that if they cannot
answer a particular query they should be able to locate someone who
can.

Potential business partners and contacts throughout Europe can be
located by using the EICs **Eurokom** electronic mail network. EICs are
usually run by host organisations, such as Chambers of Commerce or

universities. Basic services are free but a consultancy fee is charged for more involved work.

EICs can also provide information on useful EC programmes, two of which are **BC-Net** and **Europartenariat**. Details of some of these are published in the *Euro-Info* newsletter which appears 10 times a year.

Contact details appear at the end of the book.

Making use of BC-Net

The **Business Co-operation Network** (BC-Net) is a computerised system, organised by the Commission of the European Communities. It provides information on potential partners in other EC countries and may be used to find sources of further advice or potential partner companies in the EC. BC-Net also operates in Poland, and there are limited contacts with the non-EC countries of Austria, Finland, Iceland, Norway, Sweden and Switzerland.

European Communities (EC) Information Packages: scale of fees

The following scale of fees (plus VAT) applies to the provision of European Communities Information Packages supplied by the North of England EuroInfoCentre as at time of writing.

No. of employees	Initial fee — subscription & first quarter	Updating service — prices per subsequent quarter
Less than 200	£100.00	£45.00
200–500	£125.00	£60.00
More than 500	£180.00	£75.00

An information package consists of an initial package outlining the current situation plus an updating service to inform subscribers of new developments as they occur. Information packages are available on the following topics:

● health and safety at work
● public procurement
● structural funds (EC funding)

Your local EIC will put you in touch with your nearest BC-Net access point. Fees are charged for this service.

How Europartenariat can help

Europartenariat is a Commission of the European Communities programme designed to promote direct co-operation between companies in
different EC member states, and also between the EC and Eastern European and EFTA countries. The programme centres on an event held twice
each year in a selected member country giving participants a chance to
meet to discuss business projects and co-operation.

UK consultants for Europartenariat are as follows:

England
Business Briefings, 565 Fulham Road, London SW6 1ES. Tel: (071) 381
1284.

Scotland
Strathclyde Innovation Centre, 62 Templeton Street, Glasgow G40 1DA.
Tel: (041) 554 5995.

Wales
Welsh Development Agency, Pearl House, Greyfriars Road, Cardiff CF1
3XX. Tel: (0222) 222666.

Northern Ireland
Industrial Development Board, 64 Chichester Street, Belfast BT1 4JX.
Tel: (0232) 233233.

TYPES OF BUSINESS TO START

Business activity in mainland Europe (as in the UK) can be divided into
three basic categories, and it is helpful to consider what sort of business
you might start on these terms. No two regions of Europe are the same:
certain types of business are weak in some places and strong in others.
Categorising your own business will help you identify an optimum
location.

Primary businesses

These are businesses which exploit natural resources such as agriculture,
mining, fishing, forestry. Primary industry is not a growth area in Europe:
most countries, even EC ones, are far less advanced in agriculture than
the UK. The main agricultural countries outside the UK are Spain,
Greece, France, Netherlands and Denmark.

Manufacturing businesses

Manufacturing industry in Europe is characterised by a north-south
divide. In the so-called 'Golden Triangle' of northern France, western

Germany, Belgium, Netherlands and the southern UK, manufacturing is high-tech and capital intensive, such as pharmaceuticals and electronics. On the periphery, such as Spain and Greece, it tends to be based on low or intermediate technology, such as textiles and food processing.

Service businesses
Service businesses are a growth industry in all of Europe. The UK is the leader here (services account for some 60% of GDP) and the growth in service industries has been less in all other countries, even France and Germany. Service export from the UK is an important revenue earner.

SOME POPULAR BUSINESS PROPOSITIONS

Setting up a small retail business in Europe
One of the most popular business projects for small investors is to establish a shop or store in a European country. Generally, such a business is easier, and can avoid at least some of the language and marketing problems. However, it is easy to underestimate the difficulties. Tastes and fashions vary in every country and can be difficult to interpret. Competition can be intense and, in some countries, a shop may yield no more than a subsistence income.

Points to consider
- The types of shops which exist in the UK are not necessarily viable in other countries.
- Location is all important. Not for nothing do leading retailers pay prime rents.
- Reliable sources of stock may be hard to find locally, and it may be inconvenient to import.
- Local licences, regulations and planning consents can be extremely complex.
- It might take years to build up a regular customer base.

Catering businesses
This is perhaps the type of business which receives most consideration from the small or new entrepreneur. Catering includes such possibilities as bars, cafés, hotels and guest house type accommodation. Tourist countries such as France, Spain, Italy and Greece have most appeal to investors especially from more northern countries such as Britain with a less appealing climate.

Generally, it is harder for foreigners to establish such enterprises than might be thought. In most parts of Europe catering is a lifelong profession requiring many years experience to run successfully. British cuisine is not well regarded in Europe—a major obstacle to attracting custom (unless you seek to serve just British tourists).

Points to consider
- It is hard to break into the market in most places.
- Resentment or prejudice from locals is likely.
- Hygiene regulations can be strict.
- Profit margins on food are less than the UK.

Operating your own trade or profession in Europe

Those who are qualified or well experienced in a trade or profession have a basic right to operate it in the EC. As a result trade and professional people of all kinds, from plumbers to electricians and accountants to surveyors, may find that they are able to offer their service in their chosen country. The conditions under which this might be achieved are given in Chapter 2.

Good professional services are highly regarded and well paid in most countries; in many countries tradespeople enjoy a higher status than in the UK. However, the language barrier and gaps in experience should not be underestimated.

Points to consider
- It may take time to establish a reputation.
- Local laws and work practices still differ, even in the EC.
- The professional body in your chosen country may not necessarily be co-operative.
- You may need to acquire some specialist language knowledge.

Manufacturing businesses

Setting up or transferring a manufacturing business to mainland Europe has become more popular in recent years. Usually, there would be a specific purpose for achieving this, such as to take advantage of cheaper land and labour. Most countries are keen to encourage industrial development, because of the opportunities this creates for employment and for exports. Incentive, loans and grants may be available. Good transport links mean that manufacturing plants no longer have to be located close to sources of supply or markets.

Points to consider
- Setting up costs may be high, even in a low land/labour cost area.
- Utilities, sources of supply and labour should all be thoroughly checked.
- Local technical standards and labour practices may still differ.

Franchising in Europe
Franchises have become quite popular in the UK, as in many European countries, though penetration has not been quite as extensive as in Britain. A franchise can be a good way of starting a business; for a fixed fee you receive a ready-made business idea, know-how, training, support, and possibly help with finding the right premises. You also trade under an established name which should bring business in sooner. Disadvantages are the cost of the start-up licence fee and annual royalty on turnover you must pay to the franchisor.

Franchising is well established in Belgium, Netherlands, France, Germany, Italy and Switzerland. These countries each have a franchise association which may help potential investors. Ask the respective Embassy or European Franchising Federation for details.

Points to consider
● Ready-made expert help is always on hand for franchisees.
● Extensive language ability may be unnecessary.
● Franchising is not well proven in some countries.
● Expect start-up costs to be higher than in the UK.

Contacts
European Centre for Retail Trade
Sachsenring 89
5000 Cologne 1
Tel: 0221 3398 136

Union of Industry of the European Community
PO Box 21
6 rue de Loxum
1000 Brussels
Tel: 02 512 6780

European Franchising Federation
5 avenue de Broqueville
1150 Brussels
Tel: 02 736 6464

ADAPTING YOUR EXISTING UK BUSINESS FOR EUROPE

One possibility when looking for a business to set up in Europe is to adapt your UK business, or some UK business that you have a knowledge of, or which seems particularly promising. If you can run the business profitably in the UK, perhaps you can operate it profitably elsewhere in Europe.

There are no longer any technical reasons why businesses should not simply be transferred into Europe. What is possible in the UK should be possible elsewhere in the EC; goods circulating in the UK are entitled to be in free circulation in any EC country. The continuing harmonisation of product standards and qualifications should gradually smooth the process.

But first you should do some careful market research. Use the sources of information already suggested, especially BC-NET, and visit the area you have in mind, to establish:

- Is there any demand for this product/service here?
- Is there a big enough customer base?
- What competition is there?
- How will we get stock, supplies, service etc?
- How will we find the premises and skilled/trained staff we need?
- Are the basic utilities/transport links satisfactory?

Remember, just because a business may be found in every town, city or High Street in the UK does not necessarily mean it will exist at all in other countries.

FINDING A MARKET OPPORTUNITY

The fact that a business does not exist in Europe does not mean that you cannot introduce it successfully. Ideas imported from other countries have been amongst the most popular in some European countries, just as in the UK where many ideas from fast foods to motels have been successfully transplanted from the USA. The French, for example, are now discovering the attractions of garden centres and health and fitness clubs, both imported from the UK. Sometimes it takes an outsider to spot the opportunities.

The only way to identify a gap in the market is to visit your chosen region and make a careful study of what needs and demands are not being satisfied. Consider not only businesses that do not exist at all, but those which do exist but are underdeveloped or inefficient. Does a gap in the market exist because local business men and women have merely failed to spot it—or because local fashions, tastes and customs mean that there is no demand for it?

Points to consider
- How do local businesses and services compare with those in the UK? Could they be developed with new or better designed products or marketing techniques?

- What businesses have recently opened? Does this signal a growth area? What can you learn from these new businesses?
- What goods and services are hard to get hold of in this place?
- What sort of people live in this area? Rich? Poor? Old? Young? Tourists? Farmers? Professional people?
- Business services. See the local 'Yellow Pages'. What isn't available here?
- What businesses seem to be in decline?

Market research

You may need to take professional advice when researching overseas markets, either to identify a business gap or gauge the potential for transferring a UK business. Further information and details of specialist market research organisations can be obtained from: Market Research Society, 175 Oxford Street, London W1R 1TA. Tel: (071) 439 2585. Or from Export Marketing Research Scheme, Association of British Chambers of Commerce, 4 Westwood House, Westwood Business Park, Coventry CV4 8HS. Tel: (0203) 694484.

CHECKLIST

A useful procedure is to prepare a running list of business propositions. Periodically review the list and cut out those projects which are not suitable:

- Finance: how much will it cost? Can I raise the funds?

- Legal considerations: can I establish this business (especially if non-EC). What legal processes are involved?

- Licences and permits: are these required? Can I get them?

- Day to day admin: can I speak/learn enough of the local language to handle buying/selling/staff briefing? Or will I need to hire local staff to do this?

- Financial and legal skills: do I know enough about this country? If not, can I 'buy in' these skills?

- Do I like this business and this country?

4
Arranging Finance for Business in Europe

FINANCE IN THE SINGLE EUROPEAN MARKET

The European banking and finance system is in a state of flux, and subject to some uncertainty. Several steps have been taken to harmonise banking procedures within the EC but, even in the Single European Market, each country still has its own very different banking and financial system.

The **First and Second Banking Directives** and associated measures have established some common rules for financial services across the community, and for the free movement of capital and services. However, it is still more usual for investors and entrepreneurs to take advice in and use the services of their home country. Few European banks, especially non UK ones, operate very extensively in countries other than their own, although they are now free to do so.

Overall, non-EC countries, other than Switzerland, have not taken any measures to develop financial services in the face of the Single European Market. The situation is more difficult still in Eastern Europe.

RAISING FINANCE IN THE UK

With their long history, UK financial institutions are widely regarded as among the most forward-looking in the world and will consider the financing of European business ventures. However, the High Street banks are more equipped to help those simply wishing to do business with Europe, and less used to dealing with set up finance, with the possible exception of mergers and acquisitions.

UK financial institutions may finance European ventures, subject to a satisfactory business plan. The standard repayment period is five or seven years, but UK financiers will provide Short (up to three years), Medium (3–10 years) and Long Term (over 10 years) facilities, a situation which does not necessarily apply to foreign financial institutions.

Security, in the form of immovable property, is preferred to be located in the UK. Banks are apt to take a more pessimistic view of risk than for

UK ventures; a proposition for business in France or Germany will receive more favourable attention than for one in Spain or Greece. However, UK institutions rarely insist on financing being subject to their taking a seat on the board; this is much more usual in European countries.

Financing may be obtained in sterling or a choice of European currencies.

RAISING FINANCE IN EUROPE

Financial institutions in all the European countries are generally keen to advance funds for business start up and the opening of branches. Within the EC there is no restriction on the access of foreign entrepreneurs and branches to local capital. (This may be limited elsewhere, depending on the ratio of foreign ownership and any local participation.)

The terms on which business is done can vary widely. Many countries take a more pessimistic view of new business set up than the UK which saw a bonanza in small business financing in the boom of the 1980s. Some banks may be willing to advance only 30% of the capital required. Repayment terms vary greatly and are still subject to local convention. For example, Danish banks may offer loans with repayments spread over up to 40 years; in the Netherlands the maximum is 30 years. In some countries, finance for less than three years is customarily taken as an overdraft as opposed to a loan. In Spain, overdrafts may not exceed 15 days and many loans are for only three or six months, but renewable. In most cases, despite the Single European Market, security should be in the form of property in the country in question, not abroad.

European banks tend to be quite specialised in their finance business. It is important to approach the right one in order to find the best opportunity. There are industrial and commercial banks, and also agricultural banks. Most countries have savings banks, similar to UK building societies, which only finance the purchase of domestic property; in Germany these banks are called Sparkassen. Some countries, such as Spain, have government controlled public sector banks which may offer favourable interest rates.

Contacts for finance

- UK banks in the UK
- UK banks in the respective European country
- Foreign banks in the UK
- Foreign banks in the respective European country

Details and contacts for all banks in the UK and Europe can be found in *The Merrill Lynch Euromoney Directory,* available from Euromoney

Publications Ltd, Neslor House, Playhouse Yard, London EC4V 5EX, tel: (071) 236 3288, or at main libraries.

EXCHANGE CONTROLS

Exchange controls have largely been abolished between EC countries. The UK removed them in 1979; most other EC countries did so in 1990. Greece, Ireland, Portugal and Spain were obliged to do so by 31st December 1992. However, at time of writing these countries (especially Greece and Portugal) may receive an extension until 1995 and official consent must be obtained to import or export capital beyond a nominal amount.

EC regulations allow exchange controls to be re-imposed temporarily if individual countries see fit, for example, to stop investors moving substantial funds to states offering higher interest rates for investments. Banks must report movements of capital in excess of 15 000 ECU, as a check on organised crime.

Exchange controls in some form exist in all non-EC European countries except Switzerland. The Scandinavian countries impose controls only on currency exports. Eastern European countries control both import and export and only permit hard (western) currency to be exported, and then under strict conditions.

THE EUROPEAN MONETARY SYSTEM (EMS) AND INTEREST RATES

The EMS

The EMS was established in 1979 in order to stabilise exchange rates between EC countries. Under the provision of the Exchange Rate Mechanism (ERM) the exchange rate of sterling was supposed not to vary by more than 6% higher or lower (the 'wide bands') than the central rate fixed by the EC. The same applied to the Spanish peseta. Other EC currencies were supposed not vary by more than 2.25% (the 'narrow bands') with the exception of the Greek drachma and Portuguese escudo which are not included in the ERM. This position had to be maintained by the intervention of the central bank in each country.

The intention was that the band by which rates vary would gradually narrow until the EC currencies achieve parity enabling European Monetary Union (EMU). No date has been set for this although it is considered by many to be essential for the operation of a Single European Market. Until then exchange rates will continue to distort the competitiveness of businesses in individual countries. Between late 1992 and 1993 several

EC currencies came under intense selling pressure from global currency dealers, resulting in the departure 'for the time being' of the UK from the ERM, and its devaluation against the deutschmark by some 20 per cent. This has of course made the pound more competitive for British businesses seeking to sell into Europe. Many other currencies came under similar pressure against the deutschmark including the French franc.

Interest rates

Interest rates applicable in EC countries are not harmonised by the Single European Market and can vary substantially. There is a general right for individuals and companies to seek credit facilities in any other EC member state, but exchange rates and the willingness or unwillingness of lending institutions to extend credit to those in other countries still serve as a barrier to taking advantage of the most competitive rates. There has been a marked divergence in the policy of different countries as to interest rates during the recession. The UK has lowered interest rates considerably to try and stimulate recovery, but German rates have remained relatively high as the German central bank fights an uncompromising battle against inflation.

OBTAINING PROFESSIONAL HELP

Using the banks

When preparing financial plans for a business in Europe it will pay to take specialist advice. This can be done in the UK or the appropriate European country. It is often advantageous to use an adviser with offices or partners in both the UK and the respective European country, so that financial issues and regulations in both countries can be considered.

The main UK clearing banks can offer a limited amount of advice, but are more geared towards those doing business than setting up. Barclays offer a Trade Development Service which can research and identify trading partners in Europe. Its investment banking arm Barclays de Zoete Wedd (BZW) offers specialist services relating to European mergers and acquisitions.

Contacts

Barclays	Your local Barclays Business Centre
Lloyds	Any High Street branch
Midland	Freephone tel: (0800) 289359
National Westminster	European Business Section, tel: (071) 375 6071

Using the leading accountancy firms

Your local independent firm of accountants is not likely to have the information or resources to help you very far. Instead, the international financial accountancy and consultancy firms are the main source of the most accurate and up-to-date advice. They can offer advice on such matters as:

- corporate finance
- accountancy
- audit
- management consultancy
- tax advice
- privatisation

The leading practices, with offices across the UK and Europe, include the following (London offices):

Price Waterhouse
Southwark Towers
32 London Bridge Street
London SE1 9SY
Tel: (071) 939 3000

Arthur Andersen & Co SC
1 Surrey Street
London WC2R 2PS
Tel: (071) 438 3000

Touche Ross & Co
Hill House
1 Little New Street
London EC4A 3TR
Tel: (071) 936 3000

Ernst & Young
Becket House
1 Lambeth Palace Road
London SE1 7ER
Tel: (071) 928 2000

BDO Binder Hamlyn
20 Old Bailey
London EC4M 7EP
Tel: (071) 489 9000

BUSINESS ACCOUNTS IN EUROPE

Accounting systems in the European countries have always been very different; widely varying systems have long been used for presenting company accounts and financial data. However, steps have now been made to harmonise these across the EC. The most important regulations are the Fourth and Seventh Company Law Directives.

EC regulations set common rules for drawing up profit and loss accounts and balance sheets. A choice of four formats for profit and loss accounts and two formats for balance sheets is permissible. Continental Europe has expressed a preference for one of these formats by adopting a horizontal balance sheet and profit and loss accounts itemised by type of cost. The UK and Republic of Ireland have maintained the vertical balance sheet and profit and loss account itemised by function of cost.

NATIONAL INCENTIVES AND FUNDING

It is worth checking at the outset what financial aid may be available from national Governments. What are they prepared to do in order to persuade you to set up your business in their country? Within the EC, national Government aid is largely discouraged in favour of centrally organised EC aid, but funding and incentives are still available:

- Tax incentives: where exemption from tax or a reduction in corporation tax may be granted, usually for a limited period.

- Incentives may also extend to exemptions from stamp duty (or equivalent) or local business rates.

- Non tax incentives: may include preferential loans, subsidised interest rates, loan guarantees, grants and subsidies.

- State subsidies are contrary to the aims of the Single European Market and, where they exist, are strictly monitored so as not to promote unfair competition.

- Outside the EC, most places are keen to attract new business but incentives are largely restricted to tax incentives only, especially in Eastern Europe.

The leading international accountancy and consultancy firms can usually advise on national subsidies, as can the IDA or Embassy of the respective country.

FUNDING FROM THE EC

The Structural Funds

It is now the policy of the European Community that most public funding aid for industry, commerce and some public projects should be organised and distributed centrally. The amount of funding now available runs at a level of 14 billion ECU a year.

There are five objectives behind EC funding and funds are distributed principally through three organisations:

The five objectives of EC funding
1. To assist regions whose development is falling behind.
2. To revitalise regions affected by industrial decline.
3. To combat long term unemployment
4. To integrate young people into the jobs market.
5. To develop rural areas and assist agriculture.

The three EC funds
- ESF (European Social Fund). Has primary responsibility to achieve objectives 3 and 4 above.

- ERDF (European Regional Development Fund). Aids mainly the poorest parts of the EC.

- EAGGF (European Agricultural Guidance and Guarantee Fund). Has primary responsibility to achieve objective 5.

These funds now are now co-ordinated and have the collective name of **The Structural Funds.**

Projects proposed for aid must aim to contribute towards one or more of the objectives. One project can receive assistance from any or all of the funds.

The regions which qualify to receive aid are continually reviewed. By way of example, no part of the UK qualifies for aid under objective 1, except Northern Ireland. Funding ranges from 75% to 25% of the investment required and must usually be matched by a similar amount of governmental aid.

Structural Funds can be granted to both companies and to public authorities, depending on their exact nature. Usually, a company cannot apply direct, but must do so through the appointed co-ordinating body in the respective country. Your nearest EuroInfoCentre can usually find out to whom you should apply in the respective country.

The European Investment Bank (EIB)

The EIB provides long term finance for investments which further balance development of the EC. Over the last five years 48 billion ECU in finance has been extended by the bank, which works on similar principles to a commercial bank but is non profit making.

Projects financed are mostly in depressed areas. Many are associated with infrastructure projects, quality of the environment, energy policy, and promoting competition. The EIB also specifically targets SMEs (Small and Medium Sized Enterprises) for aid.

Loan repayment terms are flexible and may run from 4 to 12 or even 20 years with fixed or floating rates of interest. They can be used to finance up to 50% of the cost of a project.

Applications for EIB aid can be made to any EIB office. However, in the case of 'smaller' projects (under approximately £7 million equivalent) applications are handled by an agency in the respective country. In the UK, for example, this is Barclays Bank and the 3i organisation.

European Investment Bank
68 Pall Mall
London SW1Y 5ES
Tel: (071) 839 3351

Other EC sources of funding

Other financial aid packages backed by the EC include:

- support for SMEs and business innovation

- finance for declining coal and steel regions

- finance for research and development

- finance for education, training and exchange

- finance for developing countries. EC aid is also available for projects in developing countries, including some projects in Eastern Europe.

Further information

Further information and contacts for all EC finance programmes are detailed in a booklet entitled *Finance from Europe* published by the Commission of the European Communities in association with National Westminster Bank. Commission of the European Communities, 8 Storey's Gate, London SW1P 3AT. Tel: (071) 973 1992.

A company which provides a consultancy service on sources of governmental and EC finance is: Eurofi, Guildgate House, Pelican Lane, Newbury, Berks RG13 1WX. Tel: (0635) 31900. Eurofi are also publishers of the *Guide to European Community Grants and Loans* available at main libraries.

VENTURE AND SEED CAPITAL

The idea of venture and seed capital has been long-established in the UK. However, the situation is somewhat different in each European country, whether EC or not. The concept of a venture capital industry is established in some countries, but not in others. The Netherlands, for example, has an extensive venture capital network. In Denmark the concept exists but is limited. In Spain it has existed only since 1986. Venture capital is not available in Italy.

The terms on which venture capital is granted also vary. Typically, venture capital is available in sums between £50 000 and £300 000 or more, for a term of between 5 and 40 years. The venture capital company holds equity in the company being financed; in some countries this holding is capped and collared by law, typically between 10% and 30% of capital.

Information on venture capital, where available, and also development capital for established business, can be obtained from Chambers of Commerce, IDAs, banks and the international accountancy firms.

The European Venture Capital Association

EVCA represents the leading venture capital syndicates in Europe. In certain circumstances organisations providing venture capital can obtain further funding from the EC under the **Venture Consort Scheme**. Contact: European Venture Capital Association, Keiberpark 6, Box 6, 1930 Zaventem, Belgium. Tel: 02 720 60 10.

FINANCIAL PLANNING

The following chart may be of use in making a preliminary estimate of the capital needed to set up in Europe.

FINANCIAL PLANNER

Item	£ Estimated
Premises	£
Fixtures & fittings	£
Utilities & services	£
Machinery & equipment	£
Initial stock	£
Vehicles	£
Plant	£
Staff—initial wages & salaries	£
Training	£
Initial advertising/marketing	£
Professional services	£
Formation expenses	£
Licensing fees	£
Working capital	£
Contingencies	£ _____
Total capital required	£ _____
Sources of capital	
Personal cash available	£
Share issues	£
Borrowing from parent company (if applicable)	£
Bank finance	£
Government/EC funding	£
Lease/hire finance	£
Other finance	£ _____
Total potentially available	£ _____

Fig. 8. A preliminary financial planner.

5

The Legal Framework

EC LEGISLATION

At present there is no overall 'European law' as such. The law that applies in each member country is that which exists in each individual sovereign state, and their laws widely differ. If you plan to trade in France, for example, you will be subject to French law. However, the EC does produce legislation, enforced by the European Court of Justice, to which complaints against breach of Community law can be made through the EC Commission.

EC Regulations

Regulations made by the EC automatically become law in every member state 20 days after they are published.

EC Directives

The content of an EC directive is not automatically law, but the parliament of each member state must create legislation via its own system to fulfil the directive. This should become law within two years of issue of the directive, but often takes longer.

Influence of the European Community	
Nationality	None
Criminal law	None
Commercial law	Partially
Company law	Completely

NATIONALITY

Citizens of each EC country are still citizens of their own individual country of birth, not citizens of Europe as such. They have most of the rights and obligations of citizens in other member countries, except a right to vote and an obligation to undertake military service where this exists.

Citizens of one country resident in another are subject to all laws made in the country of residence, whether in the EC or not.

CRIMINAL LAW

Criminal law is the responsibility of Governments in each individual EC member state. This applies equally to citizens of that country and those from another member state. There are no plans to harmonise criminal law.

COMMERCIAL LAW

Commercial law—the general laws concerning business dealings — is now partially the responsibility of Governments in each EC state and partially an EC concern. There are no plans to harmonise commercial law completely, but there are some areas where laws are now harmonised throughout the EC, and more sectors are being examined:

- standards, testing and certification
- consumer protection
- health and safety
- public purchasing
- food products and hygiene
- pharmaceuticals
- competition
- finance and banking
- transport services
- intellectual property
- company law.

Further information

See *The Single Market—The Facts* (DTI). This booklet is regularly updated to give the latest information on EC regulations. There are also references to appropriate EC regulations and a contact name for the DTI official who can provide more information. Available from: DTI 1992, PO Box 1992, Cirencester. Gloucestershire GL7 1RN.

COMPANY LAW

Harmonisation of EC company law is one of the most important areas of EC legislation which affects setting up and doing business; it is now governed by at least 18 EC directives. In certain regards, the structure and organisation of some incorporated companies is to be completely harmonised throughout Europe.

Companies are already subject to many measures which have been implemented by EC regulations and directives. These include measures on the definition of public limited companies, minimum capital requirements, accounting measures, and the conditions applicable to mergers. In these respects company law is already the same in most EC countries.

In addition to the harmonisation of existing company structures there are now some new company structures (or business entities) which can be used for companies doing business across the EC, on an optional basis.

Types of company in Europe

The EC believes that the current structure of companies in Europe is cumbersome and does not encourage companies to exercise their rights to trade on equal terms in other countries. Indeed, the national legislation which governs the establishment of foreign branches (which in every EC country is much more complex than in the UK) actually hampers this process. As a result the EC has introduced a new philosophy for looking at company organisation.

In EC terms there are three categories of commercial organisation in Europe:

The corporation

A corporation is a company with over 500 employees and minimum capital of over 25 000 ECU. It is usually (not necessarily) a public limited company with shares which can be offered on the stock exchange of the relevant country.

SMEs

Small and Medium Sized Enterprises. The exact definition of an SME varies across Europe but is widely regarded as an organisation with fewer than 500 employees and fixed assets (not capital) of less than 75 million ECU.

Craft businesses

In some cases businesses with fewer than 10 employees are regarded as craft businesses, not SMEs.

Within these overall categories there are five types of legal company structure which exist in each EC country. These entities also exist in each non EC European country:

● Public limited company. The structure of and law relating to corporations (known in the UK as PLCs or public limited companies) is now broadly similar in every EC member country.

COMPANY STRUCTURE IN EUROPE

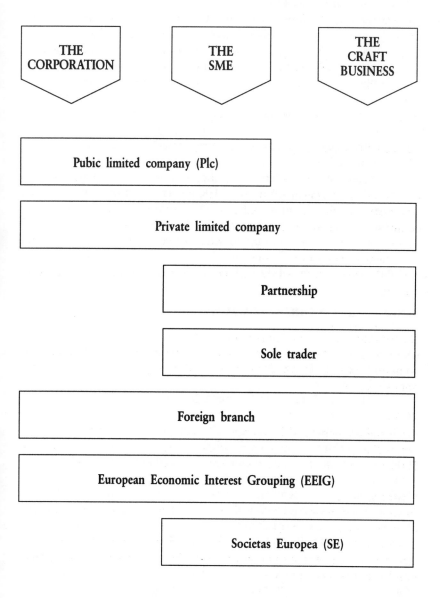

Fig. 9. Company structure in Europe—how the various forms of business entity relate to one another.

- Private limited company. The regulations relating to private limited companies are less affected by EC law. The company name must differentiate it from a PLC.
- Partnerships. In most countries (EC and non EC) there are two types of partnership: general partnership, in which all members have unlimited liability; and limited partnership, in which some partners have limited liability (but usually one or more must have unlimited liability). This format may be very rare in the UK but is more common in Europe.
- Sole trader. There is the option to operate as a sole trader in every European country on an unlimited liability basis. However, in most countries sole traders have to be registered, whereas this is not the case in the UK.
- Branches. In general terms branches of foreign companies trading in the UK are treated similarly to UK incorporated companies for the purposes of UK company law (1985 Companies Act). However, in some other European countries a foreign branch has a different legal identity to a resident company with different obligations and capital requirements. In EC countries, however, foreign entrepreneurs are entitled to use any of the ordinary business categories.

NEW TYPES OF ORGANISATION

To increase the effectiveness of the Single European Market two new types of organisation have been created for use in the EC: the **European Economic Interest Grouping** and **Societas Europea**.

The European Economic Interest Grouping (EEIG)

An EEIG comprises several organisations (maximum 500) who wish to co-operate across national borders. Organisations trading as EEIGs often do so in order to reduce the difficulties of complying with many different national company laws, or circumvent national laws which forbid other types of formal co-operation.

EEIGs must have members from two or more EC countries. They are formed by the drawing up of a contract in any one EC state which agrees the objectives and rules of the EEIG. Members retain their independence but there is equal liability between all the members for debt.

Existing users of the EEIG include research companies, legal firms, research organisations and transport operators who can then pool resources and operate across borders more easily.

The Societas Europea (SE)

The concept of the SE is proposed under European Company Statute and is intended to be a company which trades wholly under EC law, rather than the law of the country in which it is based or which it operates.

An SE could be formed by merger, or creation of a holding company or subsidiary between companies in two or more EC members. The minimum capital would be 100 000 ECU and the SE would need to register in just one EC country.

An SE is subject to the tax regulations in the state in which it is registered only, but is a legal entity as a resident company in the others in which it trades. Tax differences can therefore be exploited, but if corporate taxation is harmonised throughout the EC the advantages of and need for an SE may evaporate.

These new EC company structures are optional.

THE NON-EC COUNTRIES

Law, and specifically company law, is subject to national considerations in every non EC European country. No country has modified company law to meet the implications of the Single European Market as it affects their relationship with the EC. In these cases you may need permission to form a company. Not all the business structures may be open to foreign entrepreneurs, and you may be required to have local shareholders or directors. Foreign directors may require a visa or work permit—see Chapter 2.

OBTAINING LEGAL ADVICE

It is essential to to take professional advice on law in both the EC and individual countries. Contacts are as follows:

In the UK

The **Law Society** acts as a point of contact providing information on UK lawyers with European knowledge, partners in Europe, and European language knowledge. The *1992 Lawyers List* can be consulted by contacting: The Law Society of England and Wales, 50 Chancery Lane, London WC2A 1SX. Tel: (071) 320 5673.

The Law Society of Scotland, 26 Drumsneugh Gardens, Edinburgh EH3 7YR, tel: (031) 226 7411 can provide a referral to a Scottish lawyer with European knowledge.

In Europe

English-speaking lawyers in any of the EC countries can be contacted direct through: Euro-link for Lawyers, Greatminster House, Lister Hill, Horsforth, Leeds LS18 5DL. Tel: (0532) 581638.

See also *The EC Legal System: An Introductory Guide* by M Sheridan and J Cameron, published by Butterworths 5–11 at £25.

Further information

How to Set Up a Company in the EC, by Barry Sheppard, published at £25 by Mercury Books, Gold Arrow Publications, London. The book is complete with all the forms required and the memorandum and articles of association.

European Community Law, Penelope Kent, published at £10.99 by Pitman Publishing, London.

HOW TO GET A JOB IN EUROPE
Mark Hempshell

For a long time, continental Europe was not such a popular place for Britons to live and work. NOW ALL THAT HAS CHANGED. This book is the first to set out exactly what opportunities exist in Europe. It contains step-by-step guidance on how to find the vacancies, how to apply, and how to understand and adapt to the cultural and legal framework. Packed throughout with key contacts, sample documents and much hard-to-find information, this book will be an absolutely essential starting point for everyone job-hunting in Europe, whether as a school or college leaver, graduate trainee, technician or professional — and indeed anyone wanting to live and work as a European whether for just a summer vacation or on a more permanent basis. 'A very useful book — would be a valuable addition to any careers library.' *Phoenix (Association of Graduate Careers Advisory Services)*.

£8.99, 208pp illus. 1 85703 060 5.

Please add postage & packing (UK £1.00 per copy. Europe £2.00 per copy. World £3.00 per copy airmail).
How To Books Ltd, Plymbridge House, Estover Road, Plymouth PL6 7PZ, United Kingdom. Tel: (0752) 695745. Fax: (0752) 695699. Telex: 45635.
Credit card orders may be faxed or phoned.

6

Running a Business in Europe

The Single European Market aims to make business dealings between EC members freer and easier. But day to day customs and ways of doing business within each country are unchanged—and probably unlikely to change.

The French still tend to do business with a certain Gallic, laisser-faire charm. The Germans still mostly do business with Teutonic attention to detail. These are ways of doing things that have been practised for centuries. No Single Market can totally unify them; the foreigner must adapt!

In addition to this the EC, in many cases, sets out what will be done in member states, but leaves the precise nature of implementation up to individual countries. Value Added Tax is a case in point here. It is, therefore, inevitable that day-to-day administration will always differ in different countries.

BUSINESS STYLES, CUSTOMS AND ETIQUETTE

There is enormous variation between business styles in all the European countries, By and large, other European countries are more formal than the UK, which has partially adopted the more informal methods characteristic of the United States in recent years.

Efficiency is a particular driving force in Germany, Scandinavia, Benelux and much of France. The profit motive and sense of ambition is strong. One feature that links all the southern European countries (Greece, Spain, Portugal, southern Italy and southern France) is a more relaxed style, and less regard for meeting formal targets and aims.

A feature which links much European business is that of business by dictat—apparently a take-it-or-leave-it attitude which should not be construed as rudeness. The conciliatory view is not as popular as in the UK, except perhaps in Scandinavia.

In most countries it is not usual for business colleagues to be friends. If they are, business friends are quite separate from social friends. The making of contacts is more important than in the UK, but colleagues rarely do much socialising out of work. This is largely unheard of in Germany, Switzerland and Austria.

If in doubt, it is best to deal with people on formal terms. Formality rarely offends whereas informality can. The British are expected to be formal by most Europeans anyway so this policy will rarely come unstuck. Don't expect to be on familiar first name terms too soon.

European briefing services

Briefing courses for those going to work overseas are offered by The Centre for International Briefing. Courses are available for every European country, including Eastern Europe for which special 'Doing Business with Eastern Europe Courses' are also offered. Course content includes such matters as politics, economy, working conditions, living conditions and essential business skills. The current cost of a 2–3 day course, including accomodation, is £670.

Further details are available from: Sales and Marketing Department, The Centre for International Briefing, Farnham Castle, Farnham, Surrey GU9 0AG. Tel: (0252) 721194.

EUROPEAN BUSINESS WOMEN

The position of women in business varies across Europe but, as with many other business practices, it tends to follow a north–south divide. Generally the further one goes south the fewer women will be found in business—the further north the more. Comparatively few Greek women do paid jobs, whereas a majority of Belgian women do.

In central western Europe it is not unusual to find women in senior executive positions; in southern Europe there are very few. Interestingly enough, about 75% of women in senior management or director level posts have achieved that status by establishing their own businesses.

Women wanting to start out in any country should expect to find it more difficult than men with similar qualifications and experience. It is helpful to select a country where neither male ideas of chivalry nor prejudice make the task even more difficult!

Those with a particular interest in this subject can obtain more information from: Centre for Research on European Women, 38 rue Stevin, 1040 Brussels. The centre also publishes a newsletter called *CREW*.

USING PROFESSIONAL SERVICES

Continental businesspeople are enthusiastic users of professional services. There is a greater willingness to take outside advice, wherever needed, than in the UK where an executive is expected to have a detailed knowledge of many different business subjects. A French executive, for example, may have very little knowledge of accountancy. The main exception to this rule is law; European business people tend to be more legalistic in outlook, and a proportion have actually trained as lawyers.

Professional services in Europe tend to be relatively more expensive than in the UK; often there is also less competition for clients' business. Most European countries have highly specialist professional sectors. You may need several advisers for one particular legal or financial problem, rather than the UK trend towards one-stop-shopping for business services.

Services you may require include:

- law
- accountancy
- audit (a separate function from accountancy in most countries)
- tax consultancy
- marketing advice
- real estate
- insurance.

Further information about professional services
Professional advisers can be located through:

- UK professional advisers: they may have a European partner or associate, or be able to find you an adviser.

- BC-Net: your nearest BC-Net intermediary can use the system to locate contacts. Locate this through your nearest EuroInfoCentre (EIC).

- Chambers of Commerce and British Embassies: can often provide a list of English-speaking advisers.
  Also see Chapter 4 and 5.

MANAGING MONEY AND BANKING

Choosing the right bank
The banking system in all European countries is well developed, but in most it is not quite as sophisticated as in the UK. The Second Banking Directive, effective 1st January 1993, means that EC banks and other financial institutions can offer their services freely in other EC countries.

To date, however, there is only limited cross-border co-operation and for day-to-day business banking it is still easier to open an account at a local bank.

Most countries have a wide range of different banks, including merchant (investment) banks and industrial banks as well as clearing banks. It is important to find one most suited to your needs. For example, France's Crédit Agricole is now a mainstream bank but its traditional business was with farmers. There are also saving banks and mortgage banks (building societies).

Contact details for all UK and European banks can be found in *The Merrill Lynch Euromoney Directory* (Euromoney Publications).

In some countries banking at the post office, under a system known as PostGiro or similar, is common for individuals and businesses; it may be essential to have an account if you are receiving payments direct from the consumer.

Opening an account

Foreign owned businesses and branches can freely open regular bank accounts, on the same terms as nationals, in most of the EC countries and import and export funds without limit. The main exclusions here are Greece and Portugal where consent may be required until 1995.

In non-EC countries official permission should be sought before an account may be opened. In Eastern Europe bank accounts held by foreign companies are restricted. Foreign companies are usually required to have accounts with a bank of the country concerned; special consent is required to hold an account with a foreign bank in that country.

Regulations in Eastern Europe require that hard currency advances and profits must be converted into the local 'soft' currency at prescribed rates via the Central Bank of the country concerned. Local profits in this 'soft' currency may be reconverted into hard currency and repatriated, but only on terms set by the Ministry of Finance of the respective country.

The banking system

Whatever criticisms a British business customer may have of British banks, the banking system in every European country is rarely as efficient as in the UK; even German businesses can find themselves waiting a week for clearance of a cheque. In countries such as Spain and Greece cheques from non-local banks may have to be sent to the drawer's bank direct by post for payment; it may take several weeks to receive the proceeds!

As a result, accounting for income and expenses is more difficult. In some countries daily transaction slips are forwarded to indicate the position of a bank account, rather than weekly or monthly statements.

Few countries make as extensive use of cheques as in the UK. In southern European countries there is still a tendency to pay bills in cash. In the northern countries Giro transfer is more usual—your debtor fills in a Giro slip which he forwards to his or her bank, which in turn credits your account. The bank statement or transaction slip serves as the only form of remittance advice.

Further information
British Bankers Association, 10 Lombard Street, London EC3 9EL. Tel: (071) 623 4001.

Most enquiries on EC banking and finance directives can be referred to DTI, Financial Services Division, 10–18 Victoria Street, London SW1H 0NN.

FINDING BUSINESS PREMISES

Availability
In general, business premises are readily available in all parts of Europe (except Eastern Europe where there can be immense legal difficulties) and are remarkably similar in all countries. For industrial users there are industrial estates in all places, from Greece to Denmark, both on reclaimed land or greenfield sites. For retail users there are still independent shops, but shopping centres—or commercial centres—are becoming popular in all places, often resulting in the stagnation of traditional town centres.

When searching for and evaluating premises professional advice is advised. In most areas Chambers of Commerce, Industrial Development Associations and Economic Development Offices can help, particularly with finding property that will qualify for grants and incentives.

Costs of property
Costs of commercial and industrial poperty vary widely across Europe. As with many other aspects they tend to separate on a geographical core and periphery basis; higher rates are found in central western Europe, closer to major markets and where land is in greater demand. A distortion occurs in that Scandinavian costs can equal those of the most costly areas of France and Germany.

The availability of cheap land and property may be an important factor in choosing a particular location. In these respects Spain and southern Italy tend to be more advantageous low-cost-locations than Portugal, Greece or Eastern Europe.

In assessing the cost of property also bear in mind the facilities which are or are not available. The cost of providing these may be substantial, especially in low cost locations:

- road, rail or sea access
- electricity
- water
- telecommunications links
- waste disposal (solid and liquid).

Other considerations:

- flexibility of building to accept processes/equipment from another country
- availability of local workforce
- planning controls
- pollution and environmental considerations
- licensing
- local rates and business taxes,

Rent or purchase?

The purchase and rental of business poperty is much like that in the UK, in that industrial and commercial property is both rented and purchased. If anything, renting is a more popular option. All the European countries have a relatively stable property market, though rents and purchase prices can rise or fall according to economic conditions. The Eastern European countries are committed to the idea of private property. However, the sudden collapse of the various Communist regimes has left a legacy of great uncertainty as to legal property rights, where ownership is under serious dispute. This has not prevented rents in prime areas suddenly escalating.

Renting pros
- Minimises financial commitment.
- Avoids having to consider investment potential.
- Greater flexibility to relocate if necessary.
- May simplify maintenance problems.

Buying pros
- Incentives may be available in some regions.
- Investment potential (but property is not necessarily an appreciating investment in all countries).
- Fewer limitations on use likely.
- Property may be useful collateral for a loan in country of location.

Legal procedures

All the European countries (except Eastern Europe) offer free access to the property purchase and rental markets for both foreign individuals and foreign companies. The Eastern European countries are now committed to the idea of private property; property can usually be leased without restriction. However, there are usually restrictions on the purchase of land and property by foreign companies and individuals and Government permission is usually required. These regulations are usually relaxed slightly if the property is being purchased by a locally based but foreign owned company, rather than a branch.

In all cases whether buying or renting it is essential to take the advice of a local legal adviser. The laws of property purchase and rental are still those which apply in each individual country; there is virtually no standardisation across Europe, whether EC or not.

These are some points to consider, where practice is different from the UK:

- Confirmed and accepted offers are usually final. Neither vendor nor buyer can back out without penalty.

- The concept of leasehold (as distinct from rental) does not exist in some countries.

- Minimum commitments for rental property can be long. Deposits and bonds may be equal to six months' rent or more.

- Dilapidations clauses can be very onerous and require an outgoing tenant to undertake costly renovation.

- VAT is charged on the sale of most property (with some exceptions for new property). This includes domestic property.

Further information
For estate agents and surveyors in Europe, contact via BC-Net. In the UK contact the Royal Institution of Chartered Surveyors, 12 Great George St, London SW1P 3AD. Tel: (071) 222 7000.

BECOMING AN EMPLOYER

The European workforce
The Single European Market has done little to make labour more mobile as yet. Europeans are, in fact, some of the least mobile people in the world, and generally prefer to remain in their own local area let alone their own country.

Few countries have labour shortages on any large scale, except in some of the high-technology honeypot centres, such as Munich in Germany or Lyon in France. Most countries have a good deal of unemployment, but mainly on a regional basis. The most important issue to address is that of availability of competent and suitably trained staff which varies considerably across Europe.

It is advisable to discuss the requirement for personnel at an early stage when setting up. Further information can usually be obtained from an IDA or Chamber of Commerce. New businesses which bring employment, even on a small scale, are best positioned to benefit from aid from the EC Structural Funds.

Finding and appointing staff

Few countries have the highly developed system of recruitment which exists in the UK. In some countries, such as Greece, Portugal, and to a lesser extent Spain, senior or well qualified staff are typically located by word-of-mouth—including poaching and headhunting. This is more prevalent than might be expected in Italy and also in France.

Local shortages of senior staff may lead a new business to recruit from another EC country (including the UK) as is perfectly permissible under EC regulations. However, the experience of many employers is that expatriate personnel always expect a remuneration package in excess of local rates.

Employers not familiar with local employment conditions in Europe may consider appointing an agent to fill vacancies. Private employment agencies can be considered but in some countries (principally France and Germany) these are forbidden by law (though there are state employment agencies), unless to fill temporary vacancies. All countries have state employment agencies, similar to the UK Employment Service, which will help you find suitable personnel.

Employment law and responsibilities

The EC has wide-sweeping plans for a new social policy which will guarantee benefits and rights for employees throughout Europe. These are contained in the Social Chapter which grants 12 basic freedoms, on matters such as absolute maximum working week of 48 hours including overtime, minimum four weeks' of paid holiday per year, and minimum rates of pay.

The date for implementation of these plans is currently unclear. In negotiations the UK has been the principal dissenting voice, arguing that EC plans for a maximum working week and employee consultation will decrease competitiveness. At present, most of the laws that relate to the responsibilities of employers are national laws, not harmonised across the

Community. The few EC regulations which do harmonise law across the EC are principally related to the less contentious areas of health and safety.

Some of the main considerations for the employer, whether addressing the EC or non-EC area, are as follows:

Working hours
Vary from 37–44 hours.

Holiday entitlement
Varies from 14–35 days, and can vary with length of service. In many countries more than the statutory minimum is expected as a recruitment incentive.

Overtime
Limited in many countries, or has to be approved by the labour inspector or works council.

Pay
Minimum pay rates exist in several countries. In some profit sharing schemes and a 13th month bonus are mandatory.

Dismissal terms
May exceed the one week or one month customary in the UK. Employee notice is frequently much shorter than employer notice period.

Redundancy
Settlement terms frequently more onerous on the employer than in the UK.

Trade union membership
Single union and no-strike deals are becoming popular, but governed by local law.

Works Councils
Must be formed in many countries by companies with more than a nominal number of employees. (In Germany, all companies with over five employees are required to form a Betriebsrat).

Company officers
In some countries companies must appoint an officer (or committee, with worker participation) to oversee affairs such as health and safety, training, sex and race discrimination and equal opportunities for disabled people.

The Black Economy
This is an essential part of the workforce in some countries, especially Greece, Spain, Italy.

Further information
Information on employment conditions can be obtained through national Employment Services or EuroInfoCentres (EICs). See also *Employment Law in Europe: A Country by Country Guide for Employers*, published by Gower at £32.

Training

The EC enthusiastically encourages vocational training, although this is not, as yet, an area much affected by legislation. Generally, every European country, by convention rather than law, places more emphasis on vocational training, and injects more finance into it, than in the UK.

Few school-leavers in Europe leave without having undertaken some vocational training. The offer of a well structured training programme throughout a career is found necessary by most employers as a recruitment tool. Larger employers conduct most training in-house, whilst smaller companies can hire in the services of training consultants—a common practice in France, Germany, Benelux and Scandinavia. In many countries paid leave to undertake paid-for training is customary, or even legally required.

Further information
General information and contacts can be obtained from the Commission of the European Communities, 8 Storey's Gate, London SW1P 3AT. Tel: (071) 973 1992. The EC FORCE programme exists to encourage training with regard to the Single Market. Details: FORCE, 34 rue du Nord, 1000 Brussels.

See also *European Employent Law: A Handbook for Managers* by Trowers and Hamlins, published by Pitman Publishing, 128 Longacre, London WC2E 9AN. Price £35.

A Handbook of European Executive Training (Financial Times/Pitman Publishing, £35).

CORPORATE TAXATION IN EUROPE

Basic principles

The system of corporation tax across EC countries is largely the system that exists in each individual country; some basic principles apply in all countries but there is no total harmonisation as yet.

In 1975 a proposed EC directive stated that it was intended to harmonise corporation tax rates all over Europe in due course. However, this was never confirmed and in due course abandoned.

Member states continue to set their own systems of corporation tax and set their own rates. However, the EC will work towards removing distortions which make it easier or more beneficial to do business in one country than another. Details of tax rates are given in Chapter 8.

Parent corporations, subsidiaries and branches

The conditions under which a company trading in the EC is regarded, for tax purposes, as a company resident in its own right or a branch vary from state to state. Some countries tax on the basis of world income, others only on the income earned in that particular country.

- The EC Directive on Parents and Subsidiaries provides for the abolition of double taxation and withholding taxes on dividends paid from subsidiary to parent across EC member states. Spain and Portugal have some exemptions from the abolition of withholding taxes, as does German which may retain 5% withholding tax until 1996.

- The Directive on Mergers, Divisions, Transfer of Assets and Share Exchanges permits deferral of capital gains tax that may become due on cross-border mergers until such gains are received.

There is increasing concern amongst the tax authorities of member states where the prices charged between parents and subsidiaries do not appear to be market value rates. Such prices are liable to be investigated and double taxation applied if any discrepancy is found.

Further information

Can be obtained from accountancy firms. Information on EC directives is available from the DTI.

See also I. Stitt's *Tax in the European Community*, published at £20 by Accountancy Books (Institute of Chartered Accountants of England & Wales, London).

THE IMPACT OF SOCIAL SECURITY

Your responsibility as an employer

The social security system across the EC is already well integrated. Information on personal social security matters is given in Chapter 7. However, from an employer's point of view the system differs in Europe (EC and non EC) to that in the UK.

In many European countries the social security system is not run wholly by the state. It is usually provided partly by the state and partly by private companies, or wholly by private companies depending on the status of the employee.

In all cases social security, whether state or private, is provided by insurance based schemes. In most cases medical insurance is arranged separately from other security benefits, such as unemployment cover and pensions. It is always incumbent upon the employer to see that the employee is properly provided for. The employer may be obliged to pay some or all of the contributions, or it may be merely customary to do so, or offered as a perk.

State schemes

When setting up a business, you should register with the local state social security authorities. There may be several. For example, in Germany businesses must register their employees with:

- A trade association, which provides accident insurance.

- A Health Insurance Fund (Krankenkasse), of which there are four types depending on the type of employee.

- A Pension Insurance Institute, which is run by each 'Land' (federal district) of Germany.

The various offices will provide details of how the scheme is to be operated and insurance rates charged. However, in many countries the following system operates:

- Low paid employees: employer must pay all contributions to state scheme. No employee contributions.

- Average income employees: employer *and* employee contribute.

- Higher paid employees: contribution to state scheme by both parties is voluntary, especially if private insurance taken.

- Self employed: must usually join the scheme, unless a private scheme has been purchased.

Private schemes

In countries where state social security insurance is not compulsory (unlike the UK) or offers only minimal benefits private companies also offer social security insurance, especially for health care and pensions.

Sometimes these replace the state system for certain employees but are more usually offered to 'top up' the benefits of the state scheme as a perk.

In most cases private schemes are offered through the employer who will take out a group insurance policy. Contact an insurance company who will devise a company scheme. Usually the employer must act as agent for the company by collecting contributions and, sometimes, paying out on claims.

VALUE ADDED TAX (VAT)

Dealing with VAT
Being an EC inspired tax the system of value added tax operates in all EC countries in very much the same way as in the UK. That is, registered traders must charge VAT on their sales, but may reclaim it on their purchases, so that the eventual tax burden falls only on the consumer.

However, although the system is principally the same it operates in a rather different way in different countries. In particular, the rates charged are different and for different goods. The UK has two official rates—0% and 17½. Italy has four rates—2%, 9%, 19% (the standard rate) and 38% (luxury rate). There are no definite plans to harmonise VAT rates or categories all over the EC.

It is wise to register with the VAT authorities when establishing a business. In some countries *all* businesses must register, not just those exceeding a turnover threshold as in the UK. As most systems are strictly enforced, as in the UK, it is important to take specialist advice on the setting up and running of a VAT accounting system.

Points to watch
● Returns are to be made monthly or quarterly, depending on local circumstances.

● Penalties exist for late payment and errors.

● When a trader is entitled to a VAT credit it is usually carried over to balance a future debit, rather than refunded.

● The instances where VAT is not recoverable (eg motor cars) are more extensive than in the UK.

VAT across Europe
Trades in all EC countries are now required to keep a separate record of sales to customers in other member states, for VAT purposes.

Despite the formation of the Single European Market it is proposed to keep the 'destination' system of VAT, at least until 1st January 1997 for VAT registered traders. This means that goods shipped to other EC members are zero-rated and VAT is then chargeable in the country where they are sold, If, on the other hand, goods are sold to a non-VAT registered trader (or private individual) VAT is chargeable under the origin system, ie at the rate in the country of origin.

There are some exceptions to this, primarily mail order sales, vehicles, boats and aircraft, where VAT at the rate in the destination country is charged to everyone.

Eventually VAT should be charged at the rate applicable in the country of origin for all sales. In the meantime, however, the existing VAT systems in each country are bound to distort the internal market, though the EC is committed to removing any major distortions.

Non EC countries
All the non EC countries, including Eastern Europe, either operate a similar VAT system already or are considering replacing their systems of sales tax with VAT.

Further information
Specific information is available from the VAT authorities in the country in question, or the major international accountancy firms. Also: Single Market Unit, HM Customs & Excise, tel: (071) 865 5426.

See also *The 1993 EC VAT System: Are You Ready?* by Coopers & Lybrand, and published by CCH Editions Ltd, Telford Road, Bicester, Oxon OX6 0XD. Price £19.95. Plus *VAT and Community Law* by E.J. Hoskin, published at £20 by Accountancy Books (Institute of Chartered Accountants of England and Wales).

PRODUCT AND CONSUMER AFFAIRS

Product standards
The EC is committed to harmonising all product standards, and standards as regards testing and certification of goods and services. An EC survey suggested that design and production costs Community-wide were increased by 20%, just because of the need to adapt products to 12 different sets of standards.

Individual national standards, such as British Standards (indicated by BS numbers) are still valid but harmonisation is effective in two ways:

1. European standards are being introduced: the EC bodies CEN, CEN-ELEC and ETSI are working through a wide range of products and introducing common EC standards. These standards must be accepted in all EC countries and take precedence over national standards; products should be marked with the 'CE' mark.
Products already covered by CE standards include toys and gas applicances, but more are continuously being added to the list.

2. A general EC principle is that products in free circulation in one EC country are entitled to be in free circulation in any other EC country. As a result products from another EC country meeting their national standards cannot be barred from sale elsewhere even if they do not meet local or CE standards.

In non EC countries product standards are subject to local law. However, it is often the case that products which meet British Standards Institute (BSI) and Deutsche Industrie Normen (DIN) standards are acceptable.

Further information
Information on standards can be obtained from BSI, Linford Wood, Milton Keynes MK14 6LE. Tel: (0908) 221166. Information on the harmonisation of standards can be obtained from DTI, 151 Buckingham Palace Road, London SW1W 9SS.

Trademarks and patents
Patents
Each member state curently operates a separate patent system. However, a system of **EC Community Patents** is due to become effective in due course (the date for implementation is not yet fixed).
In the meantime inventors and manufacturers can take advantage of the **European Patent Convention** (EPC) under which a special patent registration in one EPC country gives a product protection in all the others. The EPC is not an EC institution; EPC members are all EC countries (except Ireland), Austria, Switzerland and Sweden.

Trademarks
A **Community Trade Mark** has been proposed, but at time of writing the details of how it will operate are uncertain. National systems of trademarks within every country (EC and non EC) still apply.

Further information
The Patent Office, Industrial Property & Copyright Department, Hazlitt House, 45 Southampton Buildings, London WC2A 1AR. Tel: (071) 438 4766.

Consumer policy

The EC is committed to a harmonised consumer policy across the EC, on the basis that differing policies distort the Single Market. To date, various areas of policy have been tackled and more are being considered. Those to which EC directives apply include:

Misleading advertising	(84/450/EEC)
Product liability	(85/374/EEC)
Consumer credit	(87/102/EEC & 90/88/EEC)
Doorstep selling	(85/577/EEC)
Price indication	(88/314/EEC & 88/315/EEC)
Units of measurement	(89/617/EEC)
Dangerous imitations (of food products)	(87/357/EEC)
Package holidays	(90/314/EEC)

Further information
Available from the DTI. The numbers quoted relate to the relevant EC directive.

SALES AND MARKETING ON THE CONTINENT

The situation as regards marketing varies greatly from country to country. Although most countries have advanced consumer economies few of them have the range and complexity of marketing tools which exist in the UK. Facilities taken for granted in the UK may not be available elsewhere. Effectiveness and cost of certain media is different, even in the EC.

● Newspaper advertising is important in all countries, but in many magazines carry more weight. There are few national newspapers in France, for example.

● TV advertising is rarely in as widespread use as the UK. There is little TV advertising in Germany. Cable and satellite TV is more important in some places.

● Poster campaigns are the chief form of advertising consumer products in some places.

● Direct mail is extensively used in some countries (Switzerland, Sweden and Germany are Europe's largest users) but is largely ineffective in others.

● Sales representatives. Not as widely used as in the UK. In some places independent manufacturers' agents are more usual.

● Word of mouth and reputation. Is the most important form of marketing in many countries.

In all cases tastes, customs and laws etc vary a good deal. Seek advice from a professional advertising or marketing agency.

Further information

Can be obtained from the advertising association of the respective country. Advice from the Advertising Association, 15 Wilton Road, London SW1V 1NJ. Tel: (071) 828 2771.

The *European Journal of Marketing* may be of use. It is published by MCB University Press, 62 Toller Lane, Bradford, West Yorkshire BD8 9BY. Tel: (0274) 547143.

See also *Managing and Motivating Your Agents and Distributors* by Vinoo Iyer, published at £35 by Pitman Publishing, 128 Long Acre, London WC2E 9AN.

7
Relocating out of the UK

Setting up in business abroad is one thing—living there is another, and it brings with it a parallel set of considerations and problems. Aspects of daily life will always be markedly different, even in countries with harmonised laws, taxes and standards.

RESIDENCE

One of the most important points to consider is that, although most EC regulations do not differentiate between citizens of one EC country and another, you will still have to apply for residence in any EC state after having lived there for three months. As a result there can still be differences between regulations which affect those who are resident and those who are not.

If you intend becoming resident outside the EC then, of course, the residency regulations which apply will be a matter for the individual state.

MOVING AND CUSTOMS

Customs checks have been obsolete within the EC countries since 1st January 1993. However, there are likely to be discrepancies affecting the free movement of goods for several years, whilst the Single European Market takes time to settle in.

Taking your car to Europe

If you are merely visiting an EC country on business, to visit a branch etc, there are no restrictions or duties payable on importing your car temporarily. If you move permanently into the EC you have a right to import your own car into any EC country without payment of any local duties or taxes. The conditions on this vary but usually are that:

- the car must not be new
- it must have been registered in your name for six months

- it must be registered duty-paid in another EC country
- only one car per person is permitted duty-free.

If the vehicle is new, a company car or a commercial vehicle, these concessions may not apply. You may have to pay VAT, but can reclaim it in the country of export. Even in the Single European Market this system may apply until 1 January 1997, as rates of VAT vary from country to country, although some countries may abandon it sooner. Current details should be checked before moving.

Vehicles must still be registered and road taxed in the country where the vehicle is kept, or your country of main residence. Your car must meet all local safety standards; in most countries these are higher than the UK, especially as regards emission control.

Non EC countries
All countries permit private car imports but all charge a high import duty. You should check this before moving as it is invariably cheaper (and easier) to buy a car locally. Spares may be a problem in Eastern Europe; German cars are most common amongst western makes.

Driving licences
A UK driving licence is valid in most European countries and can be used there for a period up to 12 months. It can be exchanged for a local licence without your having to take another driving test and it is preferable to do this on arrival. All non EC countries permit a similar 'swap', but may only allow you 30 or 90 days before this must be done.

Although driving licences in EC countries follow a set format, it is still necessary that your licence be issued in your country of main residence.

Further information
Information on vehicle imports and licences is usually available from the respective Embassy.

Importing personal items
You have the right to import all your personal possessions, household furniture and household effects into any EC country without having to pay import taxes or duties. The regulations under which this can be done are different in each EC country and should be checked with the relevant Embassy or Consulate in advance. All non EC countries apply restrictions to imports other than clothing and immediate personal items.

Importing business items
Business equipment, machinery and tools or equipment to be used in your

profession may not necessarily be admitted tax free into the EC. VAT at the appropriate local rate is usually chargeable on imports, although you may conversely reclaim UK VAT paid on export. Despite the Single European Market this position may continue until 1 January 1997.

Most countries allow trade and professional tools and equipment to be imported VAT free if:

- You have owned them for six months.

- You have already operated in that trade or profession previously in another EC country.

- The items are compatible with your trade or profession in quantity and type.

- You are moving to that country permanently and the goods are imported at the same time.

Temporary imports can be made without restriction.

Further Information
From the appropriate Embassy or your local HM Customs & Exercise office (see telephone directory). Also see *The Single Market—The Facts* (DTI). The situation as regards buying/selling goods from/to the EC, such as when supplying a branch, is covered in 'Value Added Tax', Chapter 6.

LANGUAGE

Do I need to speak the language?
English is an important world language and it is quite possible to get by as a tourist or even a business visitor in many countries without speaking the local language. However, if you intend to set up business in Europe it will really pay you dividends to be able to speak the local language, at least to a basic level.

Many countries of Europe, such as Denmark, speak English much better than is realised. But sometimes this English language ability of other nationalities is overestimated—not all French people speak any English, for example. Some nationalities such as the Spaniards, Germans, Greeks and Danes will willingly do business in English if they speak it. Others, such as the French, will often refuse to do so even if they speak good English.

An unofficial European code of etiquette has evolved, whereby it is up to the seller to speak the language of the buyer, or provide an interpreter if this is not possible.

Learning foreign languages
The main methods of learning are:

Audio cassette courses
Usually inexpensive, but there is no real opportunity to practise with other people. Obtain from bookshops.

Evening classes
Inexpensive, but usually aimed at holidaymakers. For details contact your local further education college. Enrolment usually takes place in September.

Commercial schools, UK or abroad
A quick way to learn but costly. They are usually business-orientated and can be tailored to your individual needs. For details see 'Yellow Pages'.

Residential courses abroad
Usually held at universities in Europe during the summer vacation. Are usually time-consuming.

Further information
The Language-Export Centres have been established to help businesses assess and improve their language training needs. Details of your nearest LX Centre can be obtained from the Association of Language Export Centres, PO Box 1574, London NW1 4NJ. Tel: (071) 224 3748.

FINDING A HOME

Your domestic living requirements should be considered hand in hand with setting up a business. In some countries accommodation is hard to find and expensive—especially northern Italy, Switzerland and Scandinavia. Temporary accommodation in a hotel can also be prohibitively costly, although both through France and Spain offer better value.

In most European countries 'living above the shop' is rarely done. As in the UK, commuting has become fashionable. In most countries there is a wider price differential between cheap property and property of the sort of standard an executive or director would live in, or need to be seen living in. In some places, especially France and Spain, the vast majority of executives have a second home, perhaps just having an apartment for use during the week.

Accommodation can be located by using:

- estate agents in the respective country. Refer to their 'Yellow Pages'

- classified advertisement in foreign newspapers

- international property magazines. Upmarket property (mainly France, Italy and Spain) is advertised in UK magazines such as *International Property Times* and *Living France*.

Property leases or purchases are organised according to the laws of every European country, which differ greatly. There are no EC laws or regulations on this. In most European countries property agents are allowed to charge a fee to a buyer or tenant (often equivalent to two month's rent), though not all do. In every country management and running charges for apartment blocks are much higher than the UK due to the different way that communal property is rented and owned.

SOCIAL SECURITY

Social security in the EC
The social security system throughout the EC is already well integrated. This has little to do with the Single European Market—the system has been well integrated for several years. The main advantage of the system is that it is portable. Your social security contributions in one EC country entitle you to benefits in another (at the local rate).

As long as your contributions record is fully paid up in any one of the EC countries you will be entitled to social security benefits in any of the others. So, for example, if you pay contributions in the UK and then move to France to set up in business you can claim French benefits from your UK record. If you then spend some time in Germany you can claim German benefits using both your UK and French record. If you then move back to the UK you can claim UK benefits based on records in all countries.

Residence for social security purposes
'Residence' for social security does not always mean the place where you actually work:

- *If running a business or self employed permanently, in a business based in the EC:* you will be liable for social security contributions in that country and not in the UK.

- *If running a business based in the UK but working overseas (such as when running a branch)*: you will usually continue to pay national insurance contributions in the UK for up to 12 months. Obtain a form E101 from the Department of Social Security Overseas Branch in the UK in order to claim exemption from paying social security contributions in the respective EC country.

- *If self employed, temporarily working in the EC, but still based in the UK*: you will usually continue to pay national insurance contributions in the UK for up to 12 months. Obtain a form E101 from the Department of Social Security (DSS) Overseas Branch in the UK; use this to claim exemption from paying social security contributions in the respective EC country.

If you are employed in one EC country and self employed in another you usually have to pay contributions in both countries (except if self employed in Luxembourg or the Netherlands).

Consider these rules carefully. You may be able to organise your affairs so as to pay the minimum in contributions for the same benefits. Contributions charged vary from country to country.

How to register for social security

Always check on arrival in your new country if you must register for social security. This may be done by your company or you may have to register yourself and obtain a social security card. For example, in Germany, you must obtain a Krankenschein each year in order to present to a doctor or hospital should it become necessary.

Some countries expect to see evidence that your UK social security record is fully paid up. Form E104 satisfies this requirement and it can be obtained from the Department of Social Security (DSS) Overseas Branch before you leave the UK.

Benefits available

The range and level of social security benefits varies from country to country, but most provide at least:

- unemployment benefits
- retirement pensions
- industrial accident insurance
- maternity benefits
- medical treatment

Some countries treat medical treatment separately from their other social security benefits. In these countries medical insurance is handled separately from social security.

Rates of benefit

Benefits in all EC countries are paid as a percentage of former salary rather than a flat rate as in UK. For example, unemployment benefit in France is paid at 40% of former salary.

Non EC countries

Non EC countries have health and social security systems similar to those described above. Deductions will usually be made from your salary and you will be entitled to the same benefits as local people. The main difference here is that your contributions record is *not* portable between that country and the UK and vice versa.

In this situation if you want to maintain a complete UK social security contribution record you must arrange to pay contributions to the UK DSS. However, these will not entitle you to any benefits (eg free health treatment) in the non EC country.

Most non EC European countries grant free or reduced cost hospital treatment to British citizens under reciprocal agreements. These countries are Austria, Bulgaria, Czech and Slovak Republics, Finland, Hungary, Norway, Poland, Romania, Sweden and some CIS states. However, this only applies to visitors rather than residents and you may wish to take private medical insurance in any case.

Further information

Can be obtained from the Department of Social Security (DSS), Overseas Branch, Newcastle Upon Tyne. NE98 1YX. Ask for booklet SA29 and individual guides to social security for each EC country.

HOSPITALS AND HEALTH PROVISION

Standards of care

Hospital treatment is considered as good as or better than the UK in Germany, France, Benelux and Scandinavia. Only in Greece, Portugal, parts of Spain and eastern Europe is it likely to be poorer.

National Health Services

Few countries have national health services like the UK where all treatment is free. Most hospitals are run privately and all treatment *must be paid for*. However, most countries—whether in the EC or not—run a state health insurance scheme which may or may not be part of the social security system. Foreign residents who pay into this are entitled to the same benefits as local people. Sometimes these contributions are made by the employer or employee or both. Sometimes they are managed by a state organisation, sometimes by a private insurance company.

In some countries those on higher incomes—though often as low as skilled worker and above—can take private health insurance instead of the state scheme, or both, or need not have insurance at all. All but the highest earners would take it, though.

If you intend using the state system you will usually have to register at a sickness insurance office and obtain a medical card to become entitled to treatment. In most countries you must make a claim from the insurance scheme—treatment is not automatically free. In others it is necessary to pay for treatment first, and then claim your outlay back from the scheme.

In some countries state insurance only covers a percentage of the cost (eg 70% or 90%). You must pay the balance or take out private insurance to make up the difference.

Form E111

Form E111 is available from main post offices in the UK. It will entitle you to the same free or reduced cost medical treatment as locals, where available, in any EC country in the period between your arrival abroad and registering for a local medical insurance scheme. An E111 is only valid as long as you live in the UK, ie until you become technically 'resident' in your new country.

PERSONAL TAXATION

Levels of tax

There are no plans to harmonise income tax rates or systems, even in the EC, and they can vary from as little as 5% for the lowest earners to a basic rate of 50% for all taxpayers. In addition, some countries tax non residents more harshly than residents. The EC has not, as yet, outlawed this. It is worth checking income tax rates before choosing a country in which to become resident. The major accountancy firms can advise, as can some banks.

It is also worth checking into tax allowances, which are never the same as the UK. Certainly so far as the self-employed and expense-account executive are concerned most countries supervise tax-deductible expenses more strictly and may permit only a percentage of certain expenses to be deducted.

Registering for taxation
In some countries it is the duty of the employer to register each employee with the tax authorities. In others you may also need to register personally. In Germany, Sweden and Denmark you may not be able to get a residence permit until you have obtained a tax card.

In almost every European country the tax years runs January–December, not April–April as in the UK. Directors and the self employed are required to make an annual tax return in all countries.

Leaving the UK Inland Revenue behind
Leaving the UK and setting up business in another country does not automatically render you liable to tax in that country, nor does it allow you to escape UK tax automatically. You can be physically resident and earning your income in a foreign country but still regarded as resident in the UK for tax purposes by the Inland Revenue.

In order to cease to be liable to UK tax you usually have to:

● be based abroad for at least one full UK tax year.

● not return to the UK for more than three months in any one year.

● be employed in work that is wholly undertaken abroad (business trips back to UK are allowed).

● not have any property available for your use in the UK.

However, personal situations vary and it is up to the Inland Revenue to decide if they consider you resident in the UK for tax purposes and liable to UK tax on your overseas earnings or not. In some cases it can take up to three years to receive confirmation that you are not considered resident in the UK for tax purposes, especially if you are merely running a branch and your main business is still UK based.

Becoming liable to foreign taxation
Tax regulations differ from one European country to another—EC or not. Some countries will consider you liable to tax on every penny earned from the day of your arrival. Others will not apply this until you have been resident for a certain period. The basis on which you can be taxed varies but is usually like this:

● if you are resident in that country, you are taxed on world income.

● if you are non-resident, you are taxed only on income earned in that country. (The tax rate may be higher in some places.)

Double taxation

There is very little co-operation between the revenue authorities, even of the EC countries. The only system of co-operation that exists is that of double taxation. All the European countries (except Bulgaria, the Czech and Slovak Republics and the Commonwealth of Independent States) have double tax agreements with the UK.

These double taxation agreements are meant to ensure that if you have income in both countries you will not have to pay tax twice on the same income—once in each country, but only in the country where you are resident or where the income arises. In practice it often happens that you have to pay the tax twice and then reclaim it from either or both countries.

Generally, those who live in one country and work in another cannot easily take advantage of double taxation agreements.

Returning to the UK

Current UK tax regulations render an individual liable to UK tax from the day you arrive back. You do not have to establish residence back in the UK in the way that you had to establish residence out of the UK.

This will mean that all your subsequent income will be subject to UK tax. It also means that you are entitled to a full year's UK tax allowances, regardless of how far into the tax year you return. Careful selection of a return date can, therefore, result in some savings.

Further Information

Further information can be obtained from your local Inland Revenue Office (see telephone directory). Ask for booklets IR6 and IR20.

Because of the complexity of tax regulations and the lack of any harmonised systems it is recommended that you take individual professional advice before entering or leaving the tax jurisdiction of any country. You should also consult the readable and expert advice given in *Working Abroad; Essential Planning for Expatriates and their Employers* by tax consultant Jonathan Golding in this series (International Venture Handbooks).

CHILDREN AND EDUCATION

Residence for children

In all the EC countries children are entitled to move and live with their parents as a matter of right. A residence permit for them will usually be granted automatically when the parents receive theirs.

If it is likely that the children will live mostly in one EC country whilst the parents work in another, the situation may then be complicated;

advice on residence should be sought from the appropriate Embassy. However, young people from one EC country have a right to study in another.

Children may usually only live in non EC countries with parents who are working or in business there.

Education
There are three options for the children:

UK boarding school
Will result in separation of the family and can be expensive. Details of boarding schools in the UK are available from: Independent Schools Information Service (ISIS), 56 Buckingham Gate, London SW1E 6AG. Tel: (071) 630 8793.

Local schools
EC citizens can use state schools in any EC country free of charge where this is free to nationals. Children will usually be accepted into state schools in most other countries, but a fee may be charged. However, standards vary and the language barrier must be considered.

International schools/private schools in Europe
These exist all over Europe and may offer tuition in English. Some offer a UK curriculum and UK examinations. Details of possible schools can be found in *The Directory of International Schools.*

DAILY LIVING

You are more likely to succeed in your working life if you fit in well to your new overseas environment, which will differ in many respects from what you have been used to at home. Here are some other important points you should consider:

- Climate—can you live *and* do business in a hot/cold climate?

- Clothes—can you get clothing to suit your tastes locally?

- Property—is local property affordable and to your liking?

- Furnishings—can you get these easily locally? Is there anything you need or would like to take?

- Food—is British style food available? Must you have it anyway?

- Cost of living — utilities, transport etc.

- Travelling to work—will you have to commute a long distance?

- Social life—how easy is it to make friends? What opportunities are there for entertainment/sport?

Plus, other matters which should not be taken for granted:

- political situation
- economic situation
- crime levels
- limits to personal freedom.

FURTHER HELP

Here are some suggestions as to where you might obtain further help, to give you the best change of making a smooth, productive and enjoyable transition into your new working life:

UK embassies & consulates
UK missions can only help with official matters like passport renewals and voting rights. Some will offer general help and advice to residents, but on an unofficial basis. In an emergency they can make arrangements, eg for hospitals or repatriation, but cannot pay for anything.

Neighbours
There are very few countries whose citizens are not flattered to have foreigners living or working with them, so neighbours can often be a good source of help.

Business colleagues in some countries will be delighted to help. In others, like France and Germany, business and personal lives are often kept separate.

Friendship clubs
In some popular expatriate cities (like Paris, Brussels, Athens) there are expatriate groups you can join. Check in any local newspapers.

Hotels and bars
In most chief cities of the world there will be a hotel or bar where British expatriates congregate.

Business clubs/chambers of commerce

Tourist offices
A useful source of information and English speaking help. Most tourist offices will be pleased to help foreigners, even if residents.

Police
In some countries the police are helpful, in others they are best avoided unless you are faced with an emergency.

Town hall
Some municipal authorities are helpful to foreigners, others resent them. Much depends on finding a friendly official in the right department!

Clubs/newsletters
You might keep in touch with the expatriate life and issues with a club/ newsletter like *Home & Away*.

FRANCE

France is generally considered one of the more promising countries in which to set up. It has a core of 55 million consumers and the second highest consumer spend in Europe, 26% of it spent on food and drink. Industrially, France is also in a good position to take advantage of the Single Market, with low land and energy costs and a 1980s growth rate of over 4% per annum.

However, many entrepreneurs considering France fail to appreciate the cultural differences which exist between France and the UK. France is more reluctant than almost any other country to surrender French standards and practices. Foreigners should expect some discrimination; it is essential to speak good French. New business and investment, however, is welcome and the Government is strongly supportive of industry.

Summary
- advanced consumer market
- good infrastructure links
- comparatively low establishment costs
- dominant force in EC policy

The economy/financial
France has the second largest economy in Europe. After the total collapse of its economy in the Second World War (1939–45) France enjoyed 30 years of successful economic growth. This came to an end in the late 1970s as many traditional industries stagnated.

In many ways France fell behind other European countries in the 1980s economic boom, although many industries performed well. France does not traditionally have the enterprise culture of the UK or Germany. The economy, still showing evidence of Dirigisme, depends on much state direction; a little industry has been privatised but the financial system means corporate funding is much less flexible than elsewhere.

French industry is much more successful in manufacturing than services. Exports are strong at 1 425 000 million FF in 1989; the UK and Germany being the largest markets.

Low land and property costs in the regions are a boon to business development, but employers point to rising labour costs, and the burden of tax and social security contributions, as a pitfall.

Business attitudes

French business men and women are determined to be winners in the Single Market. However, they are more interested in developing French markets than facilitating reciprocal rights. To some, the large domestic market and traditional French markets in Africa are more important.

Business men and women tend to have an aggressive style, which can be construed as arrogance. They are tough negotiators and push for a harder deal still if you reveal that you are in need of it! It pays to be seen as an investor in the French economy rather than a speculator; much can be done to hinder the progress of the unwary. Status and contacts count for a great deal at the higher levels of business.

Main industry/growth areas

France is suitable for the development of all kinds of business ideas. The country is a good home for manufacturing but there are openings in service industries which are greatly underexploited compared to the UK; the spend on leisure is up by a third since 1985.

Dominant industries include aerospace, chemicals, computing, defence equipment, food processing, motor manufacture, electronics, telecommunications and utilities. Some of these are the subject of Government or EC incentives, and the Government jealousy guards prestige projects, such as the European Airbus, based in France.

Small business opportunities are numerous and fields of growth include retail, tourism, property development, leisure, catering and professional services. The Government is keen to rejuvenate agriculture and offers particular help to foreign farmers or farmworkers wishing to set up, especially those aged under 35.

Setting up costs

Generally, the cash needed to start a business in France is lower than elsewhere, due to the relatively low cost of land and property. Prices in Paris and Provence-Côte d'Azur areas are much higher. Marketing expenses can be higher than the UK. Whereas a new business in the UK may take three years to show a profit, in France it could be five years.

Recommended minimum capital to start a small business—£100 000.

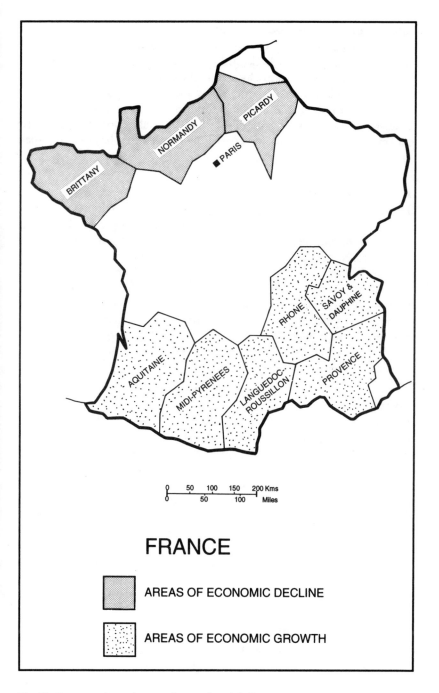

Fig. 10. France: regions of economic growth and decline.

Geography/suggested locations

There is a considerable difference between urban and rural France. Rural areas can be slow, almost backward, urban areas go-ahead and aggressive.

New sunrise industries are located in the south—especially Languedoc-Roussillon and Provence. Rhône, Savoy and Dauphiny are also hot zones for high-tech industry, as are Bordeaux (in Aquitaine) and Toulouse (in Midi-Pyrénées). Old industrial areas like Marseille, Brittany, Rouen (in Normandy) and Lille (La Métropole du Nord) often have the cheapest land and have incentives available.

Residence/registration

EC citizens require only a residence permit (Carte de Séjour) in order to live in France and establish a business or operate their profession. Obtain this from the Mairie or Préfecture within three months of your arrival.

Businesses must be registered in the Registre du Commerce et des Sociétiés at the local Commercial Court (Tribunal du Commerce). Businesses must also register with the local Chamber which covers their operations—Chambre des Métiers for tradesmen (most businesses under 10 employees), Chambre d'Agriculture for farmers and the Chambre de Commerce for others. This registration is required to obtain a residence permit. The Chamber will usually undertake your registration with the tax, VAT and social security offices.

Lifestyle

France is well regarded for its standard of living which strikes a delicate balance between modern and traditional. Living and housing costs are generally lower than the UK (Paris excluded) making it fairly easy to relocate.

The French are very proud of their history, culture, language and food. No one who does not show an appreciation of them will be well accepted. It may take some time to become accepted in a new neighborhood; in most areas foreigners are still something of a novelty.

Facilities for social life and leisure are good in both summer and winter. France is considered one of the more suitable countries to which to relocate with children.

Contacts

Newspapers with useful business coverage include *Le Figaro, Le Monde, France-Soir*. Also see regional press.

Business magazines include *Le Nouvel Economiste, L'Expansion*.

Franco-British Chamber of Commerce
8 rue Cimarosa
75116 Paris
1 45 05 13 08

Chambre de Commerce Française de Grande Bretagne
197 Knightsbridge
London SW7 1RB
(071) 225 5557

French Embassy
58 Knightsbridge
London SW1X 7JT
(071) 235 8080

British Embassy
35 rue du Faubourg St Honoré
75383 Paris
1 42 66 91 42

Economic Development Offices
Some of the main Economic Development Offices (EDOs) are:

Bordeaux: 2 place de la Bourse. 56 52 65 47.

Lille: 185 boulevard de la Liberté. 20 30 82 81.

Lyon: 20 rue de la Bourse. 78 38 10 10.

Marseille: 2 rue Henri Barbusse. 91 90 31 04.

Nantes: Centre des Salorges, 16 quai Ernest-Renaud. 40 69 27 20.

Toulouse: 14 rue de Tivoli. 61 33 50 50.

The French Industrial Development Board (DATAR)
21–24 Grosvenor Place
London SW1X 7HU
(071) 823 1895

DATAR
1 avenue Charles-Floquet
75007 Paris
1 40 65 12 34

For information on establishing in agriculture:
Fédération Nationale des Sociétés d'Aménagement Foncier et d'Etablissement Rural

3 rue de Turin
75008 Paris
1 42 93 66 06

To contact local and regional Chambers of Commerce:
Assemblée Permanente des Chambres de Commerce et d'Industrie (APCCI)
45 avenue d'Iéna
75016 Paris
1 47 23 01 11

Business data

Government	Socialist

Economy

Gross domestic product	£7 600
Growth	4%
Inflation	9.8%
VAT	7%, 18.6% or 25%
Personal taxation	5%–56%, average 30%
Corporation tax	37%–42%

Trade unions
Active in old industries. All firms with over 50 employees have Works Councils whose elected members are allowed to attend board meetings as observers.

Incentives available
State grants and regional incentives to manufacturing industry, plus EC funding. Several enterprise zones, including Dunkirk and Marseille; exemption from corporation tax for 10 years. Consult DATAR.

Business structures
Société Anonyme (SA): a public limited company with a minimum of seven founding shareholders and 250 000FF share capital.
  Société à Responsabilité Limitée (SARL): a private limited company with 2–50 shareholders and a minimum of 50 000FF share capital.
  Société en Nom Collectif (SNC): an unlimited liability partnership.
  Enterprise Individuelle: an unincorporated sole trader with unlimited liability.

Further information
See M.J. Timms' *Business Regulation and Financial Reporting in France*,

published at £20 by Accountancy Books (Institute of Chartered Accountants of England and Wales, London).

Alexis Maitland Hudson's *France: Practical Commercial Law*, published by Longman price £30.

Sam Crabb's *Your Own Business in France: A Practical Guide to Set-
ting Up an Independent Business or Profession in France*, published by
International Venture Handbooks, Plymbridge Distributors, Estover
Road, Plymouth PL6 7PZ, tel: (0752) 695745.

Marie Prevost Logan *How to Live & Work in France* (How To Books,
2nd edition 1993).

How to Rent & Buy Property in France by Clive Kristen (How To
Books, 1993).

Hints to Exporters: France, and *Country Profiles: France*, both published by the Department of Trade & Industry, PO Box 55, Stratford-
upon-Avon CV37 9GE. Tel: (0789) 296212.

GERMANY

Germany is Europe's most successful country in business. Even though its
economic lead has narrowed in recent years, compared to France and the
UK, it is still very much a model of success and efficiency. Germany is
often considered to be the most hardworking country in the world, and to
a great extent this stereotype is true!

Germany is still very much an industrial country, more so than any European country and this is a major contributor to the generation of the country's wealth. German industries produce high quality-high cost goods to the
state-of-the-art standards. The service sector is much less advanced.

The reunification of Germany, though a heavy economic burden on
public finance, has not affected the business scene substantially. The new,
high-technology industries are still mainly in the former West Germany.
There are oportunities to start up in the former East Germany (or buy former state businesses). However, progress has been slow and it is mostly
only big German companies (such as VW and Opel) which have invested
substantially in the east.

Summary
- wealthiest country in Europe
- committed to research, development, technology, training
- high standard of living, high salaries
- Eastern Germany: new consumer market of 18 million.

The economy/financial

After the war Germany experienced its great Wirtschaftswunder (economic miracle). In the 1970s and early 1980s, however, this faltered and some of Germany's heavy industry suffered decline. Nevertheless, industry is the mainstay of the economy; 45% of GDP is attributable to manufacturing. Even in Japan it is only 12%. Annual exports run at 550 000 million DM and Germany is one of the few countries to show a constant surplus on current trade account and exports are growing at around 6% per year.

Having said this, recent economic data is considered disappointing. Growth is just 2% and inflation, regularly over 3%, is worryingly high for Germany. Wage costs are high and attempts to curb them very recently have provoked serious strikes, the first for many years in Germany. Some observers consider that German products have priced themselves out of many markets; the industrialists guilty of an excess of quality.

Business attitudes

German business men and women are often considered aggressive and inflexible. In practice however they are very receptive to new propositions, but expect proof of the quality, price and reliability of supply of a new product or service at an early stage. If your product or service is not at least to German standards, and preferably an improvement, it is unlikely to make much headway.

Germans do not feel threatened or excited by the concept of the Single Market, as they have little doubt that their industry will meet the challenge. In the past, business people were sceptical of British products. Recent improvements in quality and reliability, however, have impressed.

Main industry/growth areas

A majority of new businesses in Germany are in manufacturing. Heavy engineering, electrical engineering and mechanical engineering are still mainstays, but there has been a growth in smaller component suppliers to serve these large industries. Other important activities include steel, motor manufacture, electronics, computing, aerospace, chemicals, pharmaceuticals and telecommunications.

Service industries are surprisingly underdeveloped—whether in tourism, transport, catering, retail, finance and other professional services such as marketing. Service industry in Germany is subject to more legal tangles than elsewhere (for example, shop trading hours are severely restricted) but the Single Market will help to remove these barriers.

Most new industries in the former Eastern Germany tend to be state sponsored or projects involving West German companies. Some new manufacturing industries are starting to take advantage of the east's cheap land, labour and good natural resources. Services such as transport, retail and tourism are growing, but consumer spending power is only around one-thirtieth of that in the west.

Setting up costs

The cost of setting up is typically higher than the UK. Complying with building regulations and environmental constraints can be costly. The well trained labour force comes at a price—a qualified engineer might command 120% more than his British counterpart. Minimum recommended capital investment £200 000–£250 000, less for a small branch.

Mergers and buy-outs are traditionally hard to arrange in Germany; most companies remain bomb-proof to foreign investment. German banks remain resilient to all but the best presented cases for funding, and the venture capital market is in its infancy. Most foreign banks are represented in Frankfurt.

Geography/suggested locations

The east-west division of Germany is only part of the picture; there is also a north-south divide based on the system of Länder or federal republics which make up Germany. The north of the country—Lower Saxony, Bremen, Hanover—has more old industries, which have suffered some decline. The Ruhrgebiet is also a more traditional industrial area.

New industries tend to be based in the south—Bavaria and Baden Württemberg, especially the cities of Munich and Stuttgart. There is no major honeypot city (like London); Hanover, Hamburg, Cologne, Düsseldorf, Frankfurt, Stuttgart and Munich are all important. The east's major commercial centres are Berlin, Dresden and Leipzig and these are currently the only eastern cities for which a bright future is predicted.

Residence/registration

EC citizens require only a residence permit (Aufenthaltserlaubnis) to live in Germany and establish a business or operate their profession. Obtain this document from the local Foreign Nationals Office (Ausländeramt) in the local town hall (Rathaus), within three months.

You must also register at the Einwohnermeldeamt or Local Registration Office, even if you move within Germany.

All businesses must register at the Einwohnermeldeamt also. All businesses, except most sole traders, must register with the Trade Register at the District Court. Foreign self employed tradesmen must first obtain a permit from the District President of the Upper Administrative Authority (Regierungspräsident—Höhere Verwaltungsbehörde) and then register on the Crafts Roll at the Chamber of Crafts—evidence of qualifications/experience is required. A sample application form is given in Chapter 2.

Lifestyle

Germany has the higest standard of living in Europe, a standard considerably ahead of that in the UK. Wages and average business profits are typically double those in the UK.

However, Germany is not the high living cost country as are some Scandinavian countries. Some living costs are less than the UK. Most Germans live an affluent lifestyle, although home ownership is only 40%.

Social, leisure and sporting facilities are excellent, but the Germans can be very formal and it takes time to get to know people. Standards are lower in the former East Germany but health, education, social services and transport systems have now been integrated with those in the west.

Contacts

National newspapers with useful business coverage include the *Franfurter Allgemeine Zeitung, Die Welt.* Also see regional press such as *Kölner Stadt-Anzeiger.*

Business magazines include *Der Spiegel, Wirtschaftswoche.*

British Chamber of Commerce in Germany
  Heumarkt 14
  5000 Cologne 1
  0221 234284

German Chamber of Industry and Commerce
  16 Buckingham Gate
  London SW1E 6LB
  (071) 233 5656

Embassy of the Federal Republic of Germany
  23 Belgrave Square
  London SW1X 8PZ
  (071) 235 5033

British Embassy
  Friedrich-Ebert-Allee 77
  5300 Bonn 1
  0228 234061

British Consulate General
  Director General of Trade & Investment Promotion
  Yorck Strasse 19
  4000 Düsseldorf 30
  0211 43740

To contact local and regional Chambers of Commerce:
Deutscher Industrie-und Handelstag (DIHT)
Adenaueralle 148
5300 Bonn 1
0228 104186

Two useful booklets entitled *The Federal Republic of Germany as a Business Partner* and *Doing Business in the Five New German Länder* (East Germany) are available from the:
Federal Office of Trade Information (BfAI)
Agrippastrasse 87–93
PO Box 10 80 07
5000 Cologne 1
0221 20570

Each Länder (state) of Germany has an Economic Development Office (EDO). The main ones ae:
Baden Württemberg: Theodor-Heuss-Str. 4, 7000 Stuttgart. 0711 20201
Bavaria: Prinzregentenstr. 28, 8000 Munich 22. 089 2162 2642
Berlin: Budapester Str. 1, 1000 Berlin 30. 030 26361
Hamburg: Hamburger Str. 11, 2000 Hamburg 76. 040 2270 190
Lower Saxony: Friedrichswall 1, 3000 Hanover 1. 0511 1201
North Rhine-Westphalia: PO Box 20 03 09, 4000 Düsseldorf 1. 0211 130000

Information about Governmental grants and incentives for purchasing former East German state businesses is available from:
Berliner Industriebank
Landecker Str. 2,
1000 Berlin 33
030 820030

Information about purchasing former East German state businesses is available from:
Treuhandanstalt (Trust Agency)
Leipziger Str. 5–7
1080 Berlin
030 315401

Business data

Government	Principally Christian Democrat
Economy	
Gross Domestic Product	£8 040
Growth	2% (average)
Inflation	3%
VAT	7% or 14%
Personal Taxation	19.5%–56%
Corporation Tax	50%

Trade unions
Union membership is high, but strongest in old industries. Companies with over five employees should have a Works Council (Betriebsrat). Larger companies must have a full time Personnel Director (Arbeitsdirektor).

Incentives available
EC funding plus, in former East Germany, investment allowances, investment grants, Government loans and grants, equity capital support, savings promotion schemes and guarantees. Details from the BfAI.

Business structures
Aktiengesellschaft (AG): a public limited company with minimum five founder shareholders and minimum DM 100 000 capital.

Gesellschaft mit beschränkter Haftung (GmbH): a private limited company. Minimum one shareholder and DM 50 000 capital (can be DM 25 000).

Kommanditgesellschaft (KG): limited liability partnership. Each partner's liability is limited but at least one partner must take on unlimited liability.

Offene Handelsgesellschaft (OHG): unlimited liability partnership.

Einzelkaufmann: sole trader.

Further information
Dan Finlay, *Doing Business in Germany*, published by International Venture Handbooks (Plymbridge Distributors Ltd, Estover, Plymouth PL6 7PZ. Tel: 0752 695745).

I. Sharp's *Business Regulation and Financial Reporting in Germany*, published at £20 by Accountancy Books (Institute of Chartered Accountants of England and Wales, London).

The British Chamber of Commerce in Germany issues a range of publications on such topics as *Industrial Property Rights in Germany, German Rules of Competition, How to Prepare for a German Tax Audit,*

German Labour Law, British Subsidiaries in Germany, Setting Up a Business in Germany (Series) *Pursuance of Financial Claims in Germany, Legal Fees in Germany, Security for Banker's Advances*, and more.
Nessa Loewenthal, *How to Live & Work in Germany* (How To Books, paperback, 1991).
Hints to Exporters: Germany and *Country Profiles: Germany*, DTI Export Publications, PO Box 55, Stratford-upon-Avon CV37 9GE. Tel: (0789) 296212.

SPAIN

Spain is one of Europe's bright new stars on the industrial and business front. Just 20 years ago the country was backward and impoverished. Today it has new pride; new industry, and it is set to take its place alongside the other European countries as an important commerial and business country.

General standards and business facilities still lag some distance behind mainstream Europe, though ahead of Portugal and Greece. Much industry is still dominated by the state sector and old-fashioned in outlook.

However, Spain is no longer reliant on agriculture and cheap tourism for its income. New industries have been attracted, largely to take advantage of inexpensive land and labour for manufacturing; the motor industry is a source of great pride. That said, Spain is still home to many small family businesses.

Summary
● One of Europe's cheapest countries in which to set up
● Adequate, if still developing infrastructure.
● Lowest skilled worker wages in EC
● Undeveloped 'virgin' home markets.

The economy/financial
Spain's success at attracting new business and achieving world recognition has only been partly reflected in the economic figures. Unemployment, inflation and growth figures are all disappointing. Imports in 1989 were 8 500 000 million PTAS; exports only 5 250 000 million PTAS.

Spanish industry is very segmented with some industries performing poorly but others expanding fast. Medium sized companies (around 500 employees) predominate. Currently expansion is restricted by the regulated banking market (some controls continue after 1 January 1993) and the controlling interest of the banks in many small businesses. However, venture capital companies (Sociedades de Capital-Riesgo) are developing fast.

Favourable investment laws introduced in March 1990 mean that Spanish companies are liable to predatory action by European companies; for example VW-SEAT.

Business attitudes

Spanish business people are notoriously relaxed, and this attitude still prevails apart from the top 5% of high-powered executives who work at a similar pace to the British or French . It is unwise (if not impossible) to force the pace. Spaniards like to mix business with pleasure and so personal, social contacts can be very valuable and rewarding.

Knowledge of Single European Market opportunities is by no means widespread among small business people, and Spanish companies do not traditionally look to foreign partners or investment from overseas.

Main industry/growth areas

Spain is suitable for the operation of new businesses of all kinds. It is particularly suitable for filling gaps in the market or transferring businesses from elsewhere; many shops and services do not yet exist in Spain . Services and high-tech industries are underdeveloped but encouraged by the Government.

The typical British business in Spain is the bar or restaurant. This is practical and can be started at low cost, but the work is hard and profits modest and uncertain. Competition is severe, especially with shrinkage in the tourist industry.

Important activities are agriculture (5% of GDP and increasingly efficient), mining and minerals, steel, motor manufacture, chemicals, textiles and footwear. Sixty millon tourists visit Spain each year.

Certain sectors—such as telecommunications, banking/finance, and transport are largely still state monopolies and closed to private enterprise.

Setting up costs

Spain is still one of the cheapest countries in which to set up a business, though land and labour costs are increasing in the Barcelona–Valencia corridor. Setting up costs are typically 60% of those in the UK; a small service business, such as a bar or fashion shop, can still be opened for less than £20 000,

ESTIMATE OF SETTING UP COSTS
FOR A SMALL BUSINESS IN SPAIN

Transfer tax	1 000 000	(on capitalisation of 100 million PTAS)
Notary fees (minimum)	150 000	
Fiscal Licence tax*	53 500	(annual)
Mercantile Register fees	150 000	
Municipal tax on premises*	535 000	(annual)
Opening licence tax	350 000	
TOTAL	2 238 500 PTAS	

Amounts quoted are approximate (1991) and assume the company is formed as a Sociedad Anónima (SA) and occupies rented office premises of 2 000 square metres.

With thanks to the Spanish Insitute for Foreign Trade for providing this example, from their booklet *A Guide to Business in Spain, Practical Guidelines.*

*Tax basis due to change.

Fig. 11. Typical setting up costs for a small business in Spain.

Geography/suggested locations

Spain is divided along tourist and non-tourist lines. In the tourist areas English is widely spoken and the atmosphere cosmopolitan. Elsewhere, even in Madrid, less English is spoken. Most areas of the interior are very traditional; a foreigner would find it hard to make progress.

The boom areas for business are the coastal areas, especially Barcelona-Valencia and the Costa del Sol. Madrid still carries much less weight as a commercial centre than other European capitals and is less popular for new ventures than bustling Barcelona.

Residence/registration

EC citizens need only a residence permit to live in Spain and set up business or operate their profession. Register, in the first instance, with the police (within three months) and then the Civil Governor.

Business should register with the Mercantile Register (Registro Mercantil), for which a fee, and also a transfer tax of 1% (for incorporated companies) of capitalisation is charged. They must also obtain an opening licence (licencia de apertura). An opening licence tax (apertura municipal) and annual fiscal licence fee (licencia fiscal) is payable. Registration must also be made with the tax authorities, labour department and health department. Foreign qualifications must be approved by the Ministerio de Educacion y Ciencia.

Lifestyle

The transformation in daily life over the past 20 years has been considerable, but in many ways has split Spain in two. Many poorer people still lead a very basic, almost peasant way of life. However upper and middle class and skilled people now enjoy a very high standard of living, for many comparable with France or Britain.

The wealthiest areas are Madrid, Barcelona and the Costas, as well as the islands of Majorca and Tenerife. Inland areas can suffer from high unemployment and be rather grim.

Property prices and living costs are still among the lowest in Europe, but in executive areas are no longer cheap (similar to UK in some places). Most Spaniards are friendly towards foreign residents; receiving and giving hospitality is an important part of the business method.

Contacts

Newspapers with useful business coverage include *La Vanguardia* (Barcelona), *Diario 16* and *El Pais* (Madrid).

British Chamber of Commerce in Spain
Calle Marques de Valdeiglesias 3
28004 Madrid 4
91 521 9622

Spanish Chamber of Commerce
5 Cavendish Square
London WIM 0DP
(071) 637 9061

Spanish Embassy
24 Belgrave Square
London SW1X 8QA
(071) 235 5555

British Embassy,
Calle Fernando el Santo 16
Madrid 4
91 319 0200

Spanish Institute for Foreign Trade
(Spanish Embassy Commercial Office)
66 Chiltern Street
London W1M 1PR
(071) 486 0101
Has useful booklets including *A Guide to Business in Spain Practical Guidelines* and *A Guide to Business in Spain, Company Law.*

Ministry of Economy, Finance & Trade
Calle de Alcalá 9
28014 Madrid
91 232 6124

Business data

Government	Socialist

Economy	
Gross Domestic Product	£5 270
Growth	5%
Inflation	6.2%
VAT	6%, 12% or 33%
Personal Taxation	8%–56%, plus wealth tax
Corporation Tax	35%

Trade unions
About 13% of workers are union members and union-negotiated pay rates/working conditions set the standard for all. Works Councils are not mandatory.

Incentives available
Extensive EC funding plus Spanish Government incentives, especially in Zonas Promocionables (underdeveloped or declining areas). Benefits include tax and non tax incentives, especially reductions in corporation taxes, business taxes (rates) and personal income tax and social security contributions. Also subsidies to hire those over 45, women, and to train young workers.

Business structures
Sociedad Anónima (SA): must have capital of minimum 10 million PTAS. All businesses with over 50 000 million PTAS must be SAs. Minimum three shareholders, no maximum.

An SA can be a public or private limited company.

Sociedad de Responsabilidad Limitada (SL): minimum capital of 500 000 PTAS. Maximum 50 shareholders. Capital is divided between shareholders rather than shares as such.

Sociedad Regular Colectiva (SRC): unlimited liability partnership.

Sociedad en Comandita (SC): partnership with liability limited to the capital outlay of each partner.

Foreign Branch: foreign branches have a separate legal identity; they are neither SAs nor SLs.

Comerciante: sole trader. Sole traders must simply be members of the local Camara de Commercio or Chamber of Commerce.

Further information
Robert A C Richards, *How to Live & Work in Spain* (How To Books, 1992). 176pp, paperback.

Bernado Credades, *Spanish Business Law* (Kluwer Law and Taxation, 1985). 656pp.

Hints to Exporters: Spain and *Country Profiles: Spain*, DTI Export Publications, PO Box 55, Stratford-upon-Avon CV37 9GE. Tel: (0789) 296212.

ITALY

Italy is very much a mixed proposition when it comes to business investment. Some Italian industries are outstandingly prosperous and leaders in their field—some of the biggest in Europe. Others are ailing, under inefficient state control, or dominated by ineffectually managed family concerns.

Secondly, there is a great deal of difference between the rich north, centred on cities such as Milan and Turin, and the poorer south, with cities such as Naples. The north is generally successful and prosperous and correspondingly more costly to set up in. The south is impoverished, suffers from unemployment, but is much cheaper.

Despite being a founder member of the EC under the Treaty of Rome, Italy tends to be a very insular country. Italian business works to Italian standards; little but Italian is spoken. Outwardly Italians can sometimes seem arrogant and aggressive but, once you are accepted into the community, are invariably friendly and hospitable.

Summary
- economic performance transformed in the 1980s
- good access to French/German/Swiss markets
- business methods favour small businesses
- the traditional bureaucracy is gradually easing.

The economy/financial
Economic data sends a mixed message about this country. Good performance is marred by inefficiency and decline, or vice versa. Unemployment is substantial at 12%, but inflation at just 4.7% is at an all time low. Industrial output has grown strongly in the 1980s and Italian high-technology products are now making inroads into demanding German and French markets.

Italy usually exhibits a serious trade deficit; constant changes of Government do little to inspire business confidence. However, Italian entrepreneurs are renowned for their flair in dealing with governmental inadequacies. The Italian system of small business banking through the Casse di Risparmio is notably effective in providing expertise and finance for small business. However, venture capital is not available.

Business attitudes
Italy is renowned for its laisser-faire business attitude and organised chaos. However, this is largely an unfair image. Italian business men and women are generally single minded and determined and exhibit an imaginative flair—often interpreted as rule-bending by more authoritarian Europeans.

Matters such as etiquette, dress and enteraining are all essential tools in Italian business; so much business goes to a friend-of-a-friend. However, unlike the French the Italians are not apt to be xenophobic and will welcome foreigners into their social and business circles once they have proved themselves.

Main industry/growth areas

There is no effective limitation on the type of business which can be started in Italy. However, a significant proportion of foreign business men and women enter into the growing service and high technology industries in the north, such as fashion, advertising, design, computing, banking and finance, electronics and high technology engineering.

Other key industries include steel, textiles, motor manufacture, electrical goods, shipbuilding, food processing and chemicals. Most of these are in the north. Agriculture is important, as is tourism; the latter offers few opportunities for British entrepreneurs as only 3% or so of tourists are British.

Setting up costs

Capital required to start a business is much higher in the north than in the south. In the north minimum recommended capital injected is £200 000; in the south this might be £80 000. In some areas of the north property and personnel costs can be prohibitive for all but the most well-financed business.

Geography/suggested locations

Any part of Italy can be chosen, bearing in mind the north-south split as already discussed. By and large new enterprises will prefer to locate to the north of the country, with access to cities like Milan and Turin. Border towns, with France and Switzerland, also have 'boom town' status, at a price. Rome is a cultural and administrative centre, rather than a commercial city.

It is difficult to penetrate the network of contacts and families in the south, despite lower costs and incentives. A system of bribes and corruption is still endemic in many parts. Government incentives to locate in the south (the Mezzogiorno) are substantial.

Residence/registration

EC citizens require only a residence permit (Carta di Soggiorno) to live in Italy and set up in business or operate their profession. To obtain this apply to the Police (Questura or Carabinieri), preferably within three days of arrival.

Business must be registered with the Trade Register (Registro Esercenti Commercio or REC) at the local court and the local Camera di Commercio or Chamber of Commerce, and a registration number obtained. They must also be registered with the tax office and the social security office.

ESTIMATE OF SETTING UP COSTS
FOR A SMALL BUSINESS IN ITALY

Government Concession Tax	3 500 000	(annual)
Registration Tax (1% of capital)	200 000	
Registration with the Chamber of Commerce, REC and 'Companies House'	757 950	(annual)
Notarial fees and expenses	1 900 000	
Lawyer's fees and expenses (typical)	1 500 000	
TOTAL	7 857 950	lire

Plus annual estimated audit fees of 8–10 000 000 lire.

Amounts quoted assume the company is formed as a Società a Responsabilità Limitata (Srl) with a capitalisation of 20 000 000 lire.

With thanks to the Italian Embassy in London, Economic Dept, for providing this example, from their booklet *Setting Up a Small Business in Italy*.

Fig. 12. Typical setting up costs for a small business in Italy.

All businesses must register with the VAT office, regardless of turnover. All businesses must also obtain planning permission from the municipal authorities.

Those operating most trades must obtain approval to start in business by submitting proof of their qualifications and experience to the Camera di Commercio. Police consent must be obtained for some trades, including for printers and photographers.

Lifestyle

One of the strongest reasons for locating in Italy is its day-to-day way of life. What the Italians may lack in efficiency and organisation they certainly make up for in the enthusiasm, style, good food, good scenery and a good social life. Even in business Italians set out to enjoy what they do, often at the expense of business efficiency.

The cost of living in northern Italy should not be underestimated. The language barrier can also be a problem for the family in that few Italians speak much English. Even so, the north is more cosmopolitan than the south which, in many ways, in more akin to the remoter areas of Greece and Portugal.

Contacts

Newspapers with useful business coverage include *Il Giornale, Il Messagero* (Rome), *La Stampa* (Turin), and *Corriere della Sera* (Milan).

Business magazines include *Consulenza*, and *Gazzetta della Picola Industria*.

British Chamber of Commerce
  Via Agnello 8
  20124 Milan
  02 876981

Italian Chamber of Commerce for Great Britain
  422 Walmer House
  296 Regent Street
  London W1R 6AE
  (071) 637 3153

Italian Embassy
  14 Three Kings Yard
  Davies Street
  London W1Y 2EH
  (071) 629 8200

The Italian Embassy has useful booklets—*Setting Up a Small Business in Italy* and *Methods of Entry Into the Italian Market.*

British Embassy
Via XX Settembre 80A
00187 Rome
06 482 5441

Some of the main Chambers of Commerce are:
Via de Burro 147, 00186 Rome (Lazio region). 06 679 4541.
Via Meravigli 9b, 20123 Milan. 02 88541.
Via S. Francesco da Paolo 24, 10123 Turin. 011 57161.
Corso Meridionale 58, 80143 Naples. 081 206761.
Piazza Mercanzia 4, 40100 Bologna. 051 76521.
Piazza dei Giudici 3, 50122 Florence. 055 511134.

Italian Confederation of Small and Medium Sized Industry (CONFAPI)
Via Colonna Antonina 52
00186 Rome
06 678 2441

Business data

Government	Coalition

Economy	
Gross Domestic Product	£7 320
Growth	3.2%
Inflation	4.7%
VAT	2%, 9%, 19% or 38%
Personal Taxation	10%–65%
Corporation Tax	36%

Trade unions
There are five overall unions and numerous sectorial unions. Union activity is considerable.

Incentives available
EC and national benefits mostly target the Mezzogiorno region (most of Italy south of Rome) and are considerable. They include tax incentives—10 years exemption from corporation tax (IRPEG) and total exemption from local business tax (ILOR) on reinvested profits—also non tax incentives such as grants and low interest loans, funding up to 40% of the cost of a project.

Business structures

Società per Azioni (SpA): a public limited company; minimum capital is 200 million Lire.

Società a Responsabilità Limitata (Srl): a private limited company; minimum capital is 20 million Lire.

Società in Nome Collectivo (Snc): unlimited liability general partnership.

Societa in Accomandità Semplice (Sas): a limited liability partnership.

Foreign Branch: takes a separate identity from SpA/Srl. Requires no capital nor audit of accounts.

Ditta Individuale: sole trader.

Further information

Amanda Hinton, *How to Live & Work in Italy* and *How to Rent & Buy Property in Italy* (How To Books, 1993, paperbacks).

Hints to Exporters: Italy and *Country Profiles: Italy* (DTI Export Publications, PO Box 55, Stratford-upon-Avon CV37 9GE. Tel: 0789 296212.

BELGIUM

Belgium lies at the geographical and political centre of Europe, and has not been slow to exploit its favourable position. Not only are most of the EC institutions based here but Belgians are generally more aware than other European nationals of the benefits, opportunities, and also the threats of the Single European Market.

Belgium benefits from good transport links to other countries; land and labour costs are lower than neighbouring countries. Belgium benefits from not having the strong patriotic outlook of France, Germany or the UK—Belgians can do business freely and easily and even now do not see national borders as a frontier, either in business or socially.

Belgium has suffered industrial decline, but emerged as a major centre for services. It arguably has the most developed consumer economy of any European country.

Summary
- borders with five EC countries (including sea border to UK)
- highly developed infrastructure
- well trained multilingual workforce
- costs lower than in Germany.

The economy/financial

Belgium is an industrialised country and although some sectors have declined the remaining ones are very efficient, setting some of the highest standards in Europe for efficiency and productivity; many multinationals are based here, such as General Motors.

Where coal, steel and heavy engineering have declined services have taken over; these account for 65% of Gross National Product. Belgium's export statistics are impressive for a country of 10 million; 68% of all manufactured goods are exported, earning £57 000 million in 1990. Unemployment is 11%, but unevenly spread, and a serious problem exists only in a few places.

Business attitudes

Belgians are very flexible in business and not reluctant to do business with foreigners or trade across national boundaries. Indeed, Belgium is the original 'single market', having entered into a union with neighbouring Luxembourg in 1921. Belgians' language skills can be impressive, with Flemish and French the national languages and some German spoken; Belgians are already very European in lifestyle and outlook.

Generally, standards of formality and etiquette are more traditional than in other European countries, and can seem rather old-fashioned.

Main industry/growth areas

Belgium has a diverse range of business and commerce. However, most foreign companies and entrepreneurs are involved in high technology and services. Particular areas of interest include finance and banking, advertising, business consultancy, design, employment and personnel consultancy, telecommunications, retail business and leisure businesses. Food processing and energy management are also areas of growth.

Setting up costs

The costs of setting up are likely to be substantially less than those of its competitors, especially Germany and slightly less than France. The costs of land and property are moderate and wage costs are lower than any EC country except Spain, Portugal, Greece and Ireland; the standard of living is still high.

The minimum recommended capital for a small family business (such as a retail franchise) would be perhaps £80 000. A small service business (for example, a printing works) would probably require at least £150 000.

Geography/suggested locations

Industry and commerce is well spread across Belgium, a small country of only 11 800 square miles; Brussels is not a honeypot capital as such.

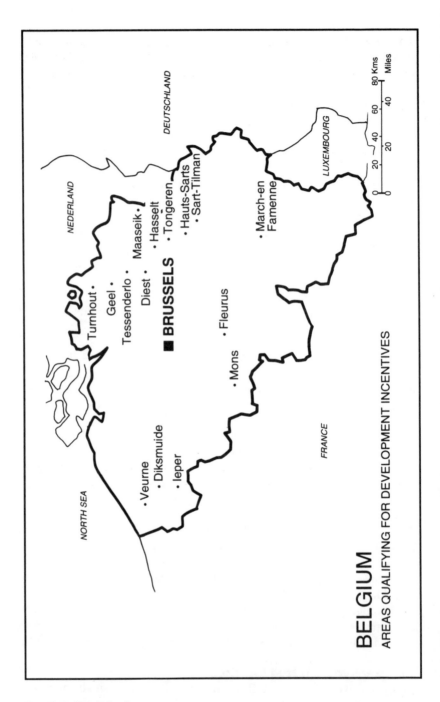

Fig. 13. Belgium: development areas

There are principally three regions—Flanders in the north, Brussels (central) and Wallonia in the south; both Flanders and Wallonia have suffered from the industrial decline and qualify for most relocation incentives.

Residence/registration

EC citizens require only a residence card in order to live in Belgium and establish a business or operate their profession. You will need to obtain this from the town hall of the Commune where you wish to live within six months of arrival. After six months you will receive a Belgian identity card which can be used, like a passport, to travel anywhere in the EC.

Businesses, whether resident or branches, must be registered in the Trade Register and obtain a registration number. This is done at the local Tribunal du Commerce or Handelsrechtbank (Commercial Court). Prior to this those engaged in a trade must obtain a permit, given on proof of skills/qualifications, from the Chambre des Métiers et Négoces (Chamber of Crafts and Trades).

Planning permission must be sought from the local Commune before establishing a new venture or before changing existing manufacturing processes.

Lifestyle

Belgium has a very high standard of living and this applies to the vast majority of employees and business people. Ownership of cars and domestic appliances is among the highest in Europe, although home ownership is less than the UK. Consumer services, such as retail, banking and finance, are extremely sophisticated.

Belgians are used to dealing with foreigners and, as there are so many expatriates everywhere there is little sign of an insular attitude, as there might be elsewhere. It is easier for other nationals to become accepted than elsewhere, although Belgians are formal at first.

Contacts

Newspapers with useful business coverage include *De Morgen* and *Le Soir*.

Those wishing to set up in business may find the expatriate magazines *Newcomer*, *The Bulletin*, *Prospects 92* and *Business Journal* useful. Published by Ackroyd Publications, 329 Avenue Molière, 1060 Brussels. Tel: 02 343 99 09.

British Chamber of Commerce
  30 rue Joseph II
  1040 Brussels
  02 219 07 88

Belgo-Luxembourg Chamber of Commerce in Great Britain
  36 Piccadilly
  London W1R 7TH
  (071) 434 1815

Belgian Embassy
  103 Eaton Square
  London SW1W 9AB
  (071) 235 5422

British Embassy
  Britannia House
  28 rue Joseph II
  1040 Brussels
  02 217 90 00

Brussels Chamber of Commerce
  Avenue Louise 500
  1050 Brussels
  02 648 50 02

Economic Development Offices (EDOs):
  Brussels region: Rue Royale 2, 1000 Brussels. 02 518 17 11.
  Flanders region: Avenue de l'Astronomie 21, 1040 Brussels. 02 219
  25 90.
  Wallonia region: Boulevard de l'Empereur 11, 1000 Brussels. 02 511
  72 95.

Business data

Government   Coalition Christian/Socialist

Economy
Gross Domestic Product   £7 130
Growth   4.2%
Inflation   3%
VAT   1%, 6%, 17%, 19%, 25% or 33%
Personal taxation   25%–72%
Corporation tax   43%

Trade unions
Unions negotiate minimum wages and conditions of employment which
are then usually adopted as the norm for all employees, members or not.
Companies with over 100 employers must have a Works Council (Conseil
d'entreprise/Ondernemingsraad).

Incentives available
EC funding plus extensive Government support including tax exemptions, tax holidays, loan interest rebates and loan guarantees. Mainly available in areas designated T-Zones (Employment Zones) and Development Areas. These are at Veurne, Diksmunde, Ieper, Turnhout, Maaseik, Hasselt, Tongeren, Geel, Tessenderlo, Diest, Hauts-Sarts, Sart-Tilman, Marche-en-Famenne, Fleurus and Mons.

Business structures
Société Anonyme (SA)/Naamloze Vennootschap (NV): a corporation with at least two shareholders and BEF 1 250 000 capital.

Société Privée à Responsabilité Limitée (SPRL)/Besloten Vennootschap met Beperkte Aansprakelijkheid (BVBA): a limited liability company. Minimum BEF 750 000 capital, of which BEF 250 000 has to be paid up.

Société en Non Collectif (SNC)/Vennootschap Onder Firma (VOF): general partnership with unlimited liability.

Société en Commandite Simple (SCS)/Gewone Commanditaire Vennootschap (GCV): limited liability partnership.

Société en Commandite par Actions (SCA)/Commanditaire Vennootschap op Aandelen (CVA): partnership limited by shares.

Société Coopérative (SC)/Cooperatieve Vennootschap (CV): a co-operative company.

Sole Trader: sole traders in Belgium are often, instead, one-member limited liability companies (SPRLs/BVBAs).

Further information
Marvina Shilling, *How to Live & Work in Belgium* (How To Books, 1991). Paperback.

Hints to Exporters: Belgium and *Country Profiles: Belgium* (DTI Export Publications PO Box 55, Stratford-upon-Avon CV37 9GE. Tel: 0789 296212).

THE NETHERLANDS

The Netherlands has long maintained an internationalist policy. It enthusiastically promoted links with other countries, and foreign investment, long before the EC or the Single European Market came into being. The Netherlands relies on this international trade for its economic success.

Enterprise culture is not, like in the UK, a phenomenon born in the 1980s to the Dutch. The Dutch have long recognised the need to be enterprising to earn a living. Amsterdam may be overshadowed by London on the financial markets, but rivals it as a world trading centre.

Regulation of business, though adequate, has long been less than in other countries and it has always been easy for foreigners to start up here. By and large the Dutch are outgoing towards other nationalities and welcome business links, trading partnerships and mutual investment, rather than resenting it as in some other countries.

Summary
- long established trading links worldwide
- solid industrial base; high technology/services well established
- good infrastructure
- minimal regulation of business; less red tape than most of continental Europe.

The economy/financial

The Netherlands economy benefits from a stable and reliable political system that has proved attractive to business and investment over the years. It is a country which not only promotes free enterprise, but enterprise is ingrained in the culture. State corporations are few and restrictions on business are not comprehensive.

Notable features of the Dutch economy are continuous low inflation and a constant balance of payments surplus. Unemployment has been considered a problem but is two-thirds of that in most competitor countries. Dutch companies show the highest rate of return on capital in Europe, and amongst the highest productivity. However, exports as a percentage of GDP (59%) have been falling and are no longer the European leader.

Business attitudes

The Dutch attitude towards business is very positive and all propositions offering gain are likely to be enthusiastically pursued. Like the Belgians, national borders are rarely seen as a barrier and patriotism does not cloud business dealings, as it can in France. Many executives will happily speak English.

In many respects business methods are similar to Britain; formality on meeting soon gives way to informality. Business men and women can be down-to-earth or even blunt.

Main industry/growth areas

The industrial base of the Netherlands is very solidly established and industrial decline has been less of a problem than elsewhere. However, new high technology industries and services are taking over. The Netherlands industrial scene is dominated by large corporations; and a large percentage of the plethora of family businesses are their suppliers and contractors.

Growth areas include agriculture, food production and processing, light engineering, electronics, computers, medical equipment, printing, high technology chemicals including agro-chemicals, shipping, aerospace, transport and communications services, tourism, accountancy, marketing and market research.

Setting up costs

Costs of setting up a business in the Netherlands are likely to be less than in comparable European countries such as the UK and Germany. Land, property and running costs are all moderate; the threat of unemployment has moderated what were spiralling wage rates. Minimum suggested capital: £120 000.

Dutch and foreign banks trading in the Netherlands offer highly flexible industrial financing facilities. Venture capital is used extensively, as is capital provision through private participation companies known as PPMs.

Geography/suggested locations

Industry and commerce is well spread across the Netherlands, although the most industrialised area is the west—largely an area bounded by the cities of Amsterdam, The Hague, Rotterdam and Utrecht. Most service businesses or those connected with international trade and high technology gravitate around Amsterdam. However, there has also been a rash of development in the towns along the German border, such as Enschede and Nijmegen.

Residence/registration

EC citizens require only a residence permit in order to live in the Netherlands and establish a business or operate their profession. This should be obtained from the nearest Aliens Authority or police station, preferably within eight days of arrival.

Application to form an incorporated company must be made to the Ministry of Justice and a 'Certificate of No Objection' obtained. All other businesses must register with the Commercial Trade Register (Handelsregister) at the local Chamber of Commerce and Industry (Kamer van Koophandel en Fabrieken). Certain trades and professions require approval by the Chamber, and proof of skills/qualifications, otherwise it is merely a formality. The application form appears in Chapter 2.

Lifestyle

The Netherlands has one of the highest standards of living in Europe—some way between that in the UK and Germany. Levels of ownership of material goods, such as cars, household appliances and the like are very high, promoted by comparatively low daily living costs.

The Netherlands is also one of the most cosmopolitan countries. Foreigners are readily accepted and many people speak some English. A knowledge of Dutch is always recommended for business but some people manage without knowing very much at all. The Dutch outlook on life—as well as the political system and monarchy—is not too far removed from that in the UK.

Contacts

Newspapers with useful business coverage include *De Telegraaf, De Volkskrant, Het Parool,* and *Haagsche Courant.*

Netherlands-British Chamber of Commerce
  Bezuidenhoutsweg 181
  2594 AH The Hague
  070 478881

Netherlands-British Chamber of Commerce
  307–308 High Holborn
  London WC1V 7LS
  (071) 405 1538

Royal Netherlands Embassy
  38 Hyde Park Gate
  London SW7 5DP
  (071) 584 5040

British Embassy
  Lange Voorhout 10
  2514 ED The Hague
  070 364 5800

Some of the main Chambers of Commerce are:
  Amsterdam: Koningen Wilheminaplein 13. Tel: 020 172882.
  Rotterdam: Postbus 30 025. Tel: 010 145022.
  The Hague: Alexander Gogelweg 16. Tel: 070 614101.

Business data

Government	Centre-left coalition

Economy

Gross Domestic Product	£7 250
Growth	3.5%
Inflation	1.3%
VAT	6% or 18.5%
Personal taxation	14%–60% plus wealth tax
Corporation tax	35%–40%

Trade unions

Union membership is 30%, but compulsory in a very few industries. Union-employer relations are traditionally good and not confrontational as in other countries. Companies with over 35 employees must have a Works Council which must be kept informed of board decisions. A minimum wage applies to employees over 23.

Incentives available

EC and national benefits target both underdeveloped regions and industries which have been selected for development under the PBTS scheme. The areas which receive most incentives are Groningen, Friesland, Drente, Twente, Lelystad, Arnhem, Beuningen, Nijmegen, Wijchen, Aarle-Rixen, Bakel, Milheeze, Helmond, Mierlo and South Limburg. PBTS scheme sectors are information technology, biotechnology, medical technology and advanced materials technology.

Both tax and non tax incentives are available but in the regions grants, low interest loans and Government equity capital are available.

Business structures

Naamloze Vennootschap (NV): a public limited company. Minimum capital is DFL 100 000.

Besloten Vennootschap met Beperkte Aansprakelijkheid (BV): a private limited company. Minimum capital is DFL 40 000. BVs do not have to file their accounts as private companies do in the UK.

Vennootschap onder Firma (VoF): general partnership, unlimited liability.

Commanditaire Vennootschap (CV): limited partnership.

Eenmanszaak: sole trader.

Further information

Hints to Exporters: Netherlands and *Country Profiles: Netherlands* (DTI Export Publications, PO Box 55, Stratford-upon-Avon CV37 9GE. Tel: 0789 296212).

GREECE

Greece, though now a member of the EC, has always been a very independently minded country and does not always fit neatly alongside the other EC member states. The language obstacle and the generally different Greek way of looking at things has kept the country at the periphery of Europe; it is not a country that has 'Europeanised' to the same extent as Spain.

However, Greece is a very entrepreneurial minded country. Small enterprises flourish in most small towns unfettered by excessive bureaucracy—Greeks do not bother too much about rules—and promoted by the cost of land and labour which is among the lowest in the EC. Much new industry has been attracted on this basis and the widening gap between this country and the more industrialised EC countries may change all that, although the infrastructure and distance to EC markets are a drawback.

Summary
- government emphasis has always been on private ownership
- low land and labour costs
- government keen to encourage new industry
- commitment to simplify the complex bureaucracy.

The economy/financial
During the 1970s the Greek economy enjoyed a period of intense growth and development but this came to an end in 1978–79. A failure to develop modern industry and the crippling costs of imported energy were held responsible. Tough economic measures were taken to remedy the situation.

By the mid 1980s the benefits of Greece's membership of the EC started to come on line; EC aid was used to good effect and new markets in the EC began to be exploited. However, the gap between imports and exports (880 000 million Drachmas in 1990) is still widening.

The financial system has been simplified and streamlined in recent years and financing through commercial banks, investment banks and special credit organisations is available. Venture capital is offered.

Business attitudes
The Greek attitude to business is distinctly relaxed. Most businessmen (there are few women) like to mix business with pleasure and business with friendships. The entrepreneurial spirit is strong, with a tendency to wheeler-dealing.

Few Greek businessmen know much about the Single European Market, or are well prepared to take advantage of it. By and large it is far easier to set up a business which buys from Greek suppliers, than one which exploits the Greek market.

Main industry/growth areas
Good natural resources, cheap land and labour are the keystones of most new development. Basic manufacturing industry is expected to grow. This includes principally clothing, textiles, footwear, chemicals, mining and minerals and food processing. However, most industry remains low and medium technology. Services in shipping and trade, banking and finance have always been important. The growth in tourism has slowed down; unlike Spain comparatively few foreigners have sufficient knowledge of this market or the language to start small businesses in tourism.

Setting up costs
Start up costs are some of the lowest in Europe, although infrastructure costs—supplying basic services such as roads, electricity and reliable water—can be high. There is a marked difference between Athens and the provinces and islands. A West German company was recently reported to have established a small (20 workers) clothing manufacturing plant in Thessaloniki for little over £80 000 equivalent.

Geography/suggested locations
Athens is the only centre for major commercial and service businesses. The traffic and pollution are notorious. Most manufacturing plants tend to locate in a triangle bordered by Athens, Corinth and Larisa. Thessaloniki (Salonica) is also something of a boom area for new industry. Most tourism is on the islands; new resorts are being continuously opened up, but usually on a very small scale.

Residence/registration
EC citizens require only a residence permit (a 'blue card') in order to live in Greece and establish a business or operate their profession. This should be obtained from the nearest main police station.

Incorporated companies require permission to trade from the Ministry of Commerce; if a foreign branch also from the Ministry of National Economy (a formality for EC companies). Partnerships must have their partnership agreement registered with the District Court.

All business must obtain an operating permit from the local office of the Ministry of Labour. Those operating most trades and professions must obtain permission from the Ministry for Industry and Energy. The acceptance of foreign professional qualifications is still in a transitional phase.

Finally, businesses must register with the local Chamber of Commerce. Numerous other permits (health permits, technical permits etc) are required and, as few foreigners have sought these as yet, it is best to seek the assistance of the Chamber. A sample application form appears in Chapter 2.

Lifestyle

Greece is generally considered to have an appealing an attractive way of life. Only Athens and district could be described as industrialised and offering a big-city lifestyle. The city is cosmopolitan with good facilities but crowded, noisy, congested, polluted and extremely hot in summer.

Out in the regions and islands the pace of life is invariably slow. It is often difficult to get things done and facilities and standards of local services are very basic. Depite the influx of mass tourism to Greece there are still plenty of islands and inland areas where tourists have not penetrated and where foreigners would feel very isolated.

Contacts

British-Hellenic Chamber of Commerce
25 Vas Sofias Avenue
10674 Athens
01 721 0361

Greek Embassy
la Holland Park
London W11 3TP
(071) 727 8040

British Embassy
1 Ploutarchou Street
10675 Athens
01 723 6211

Ministry for Industry and Energy
Directorate-General 1
Odos Michalakopoulou 80
Athens

Ministry for Northern Greece
Odos Venizelou 48
Thessaloniki
031 264321

Business data

Government	Socialist

Economy

Gross Domestic Product	£3 810
Growth	2%
Inflation	5.7%
VAT	3%, 6%, 16% or 36%
Personal taxation	8%–50%
Corporation tax	46%

Trade unions
Trade unions have extensive membership in some sectors, but little in those which are mainly comprised of small businesses. Works Councils were introduced in 1988; all companies with 50 or more employees must form them.

Incentives available
Extensive EC funding, partly under the Integrated Mediterranean Programme (IMP) and complex system of national tax and non tax incentives. Incentives are sectoral rather than regional and apply especially to manufacturing industries, mining, hotel and tourism developments, agriculture, livestock, fishing and shipping.

Business structures
Anonymos Eteria (AE) or Société Anonyme (SA): a public limited company. Minimum capital of 5 million Drachmas.
  Eteria Periorismenis Efthinis (EPE): private limited company. Minimum capital 200 000 Drachmas and two shareholders.
  Ipokatastima Xenis Eterias (IXE): foreign branch.
  Omorythmos Eteria (OE): general partnership, unlimited liability.
  Eterorythmos Eteria (EE): limited liability partnership.
  Kinopraxia: joint venture.
  Atomiki Epihirisi: sole trader.

Further information
Hints to Exporters: Greece and *Country Profiles: Greece* (DTI Export Publications, PO Box 55, Stratford-upon-Avon CV39 9GE. Tel: 0789 296212).

PORTUGAL

Portugal is the poorest country in the EC and the gulf between it and the richest, such as Germany and the UK, is considerable. Attempts to bring Portugal more into mainstream Europe have been partially successful, but the transformation brought through EC membership has not been as outstanding as that in Spain. The economic gap between Spain and Portugal is wider than ever.

But Portugal has many things in its favour, being by far the cheapest place in the EC to set up. The consumer market is perhaps 20 years behind the UK, offering attendant business opportunities. The trading links between Britain and Portugal go back several hundred years and Portugal has more regard for the UK than any other EC country.

Summary
● cheap land and labour
● links with Europe, through Spain, being improved
● manufacturing industry encouraged.

The economy/financial
The economy of Portugal is small when compared to other countries. Gross Domestic Product (GDP) is less than half that in the UK. Unemployment and inflation are perennial problems and most of the key industries are controlled by a very small number of private individuals.

But Portugal has made great strides, bearing in mind it was a country in revolution in 1974, and only joined the EC in 1986. Traditional industries have been turned round with some success to serve new markets; exports in 1989 were £7 738 000 million. UK companies have over 7% of the Portuguese market, and the UK is becoming Portugal's single largest market.

Business attitudes
Business attitudes in Portugal are quite distinct from those in Spain—and in no circumstances should the countries be confused. Portuguese executives tend to be less relaxed, certainly more formal and, where local conditions permit, reasonably efficient. It is easy to forget that Portugal is not a Mediterranean country, and so does not share a Mediterranean outlook.

Few Portuguese businessmen (there are few women) are well informed on the Single European Market. However, most know that their low costs of production are their country's major selling point.

Main industry/growth areas

Portugal is principally a base for low cost agriculture and low cost manufacturing. These may be areas of decline in some countries, but are expanding here. Agriculture has been modernised to some extent. Food processing and motor manufacture are flagship industries. The traditional industries in clothing, textiles and footwear are growing fast. Other activities include chemicals, timber, electrical manufacture, light engineering and shipbuilding.

Services are not much in evidence, but the Algarve does have a fair number of British bars, restaurants, and real estate agencies—usually more up-market than in Spain.

Setting up costs

These are the lowest anywhere in the EC, though expect to pay more in Lisbon. The cost of providing basic services may be high in places where they do not already exist. Labour costs are low—a competent Portuguese manager can be hired for the equivalent of £10 000 a year—but trained staff may be hard to find outside Lisbon. It has been estimated that a small manufacturing plant (textiles) costing £300 000 to set up in the UK would require only £120 000 in provincial Portugal.

Sources of local capital are limited and local banks and financial institutions are unused to financing large projects.

Geography/suggested locations

Much of Portugal is isolated and culturally very remote compared to the rest of Europe. It would be difficult for any business man or woman without a thorough knowledge of Portugal to establish in most places.

A manufacturing business should base itself in Lisbon or Oporto; service and commercial activities in Lisbon only. Tourist type businesses are only likely to thrive on the Algarve (Faro, Albufeira, Lagos); tourist trade elsewhere, even at Estoril near Lisbon, is small.

Residence/registration

EC citizens require only a residence permit (authorização de residência) in order to live in Portugal and establish a business or operate their profession. This should be obtained from the nearest Aliens Authority office.

Businesses must be registered with the Register of Enterprises (Cadastro Industrial), at the local Commercial Court (Tribunais de Comércio). They must also obtain an operating permit or trading authorisation from the local municipal authorities. As Portuguese exchange controls have not been fully abandoned permission for foreign investment (from the

Institute for Foreign Investment) and to import capital (from the Banco de Portugal) must be obtained.

Very few trades in Portugal (such as electricians) currently require proof of professional qualifications to operate.

Lifestyle

By and large Portugal offers a slow pace of life, beautiful scenery and superb weather and this is its major selling point. Lisbon and Oporto are the only major industrial centres; elsewhere is unspoiled. Even the Algarve has not really been spoiled by development.

Prices in Lisbon and the tourist spots are inflated. Elsewhere land, property and daily living costs are tiny by European standards. In Lisbon and the Algarve a modern way of life can be enjoyed—£70 000 or £80 000 will buy a luxury executive property—but elsewhere it may be quite basic and would take some considerable readjustment.

Contacts

Newspapers with useful business coverage include *O Diario*.

British-Portuguese Chamber of Commerce
  Rua da Estrella 8
  1200 Lisbon
  01 661586

  Also:
  Rua Sa de Bandeira 784–20E
  Frente
  4000 Oporto

Portuguese Chamber of Commerce in the UK
  New Bond Street House
  New Bond Street
  London W1Y 9PE
  (071) 493 9973

Portuguese Embassy
  11 Belgrave Square
  London SW1X 8PP
  (071) 235 5331

British Embassy
  35–37 Rua de S. Domingos à Lapa
  1200 Lisbon
  01 396 1191

Institute for Foreign Investment
Avenida da Liberdade 258–5
1200 Lisbon

Some of the main Chambers of Commerce:
Lisbon: Rua de Santo Antonio 88. Tel: 01 327289.
Oporto: Palacio da Bolsa. Tel: 02 24497.

Business data

Government	Social Democratic

Economy

Gross Domestic Product	£3 550
Growth	1%
Inflation	6.7%
VAT	8%, 16% or 30%
Personal taxation	4.8%–60%
Corporation tax	36.5%

Trade unions
Union activity is not considerable, especially amongst the small family businesses that are common. Works Councils are being introduced by larger employers.

Incentives available
National benefits, plus most EC benefits available in Portugal. Sectors targeted are infrastructure, light manufacturing, and most areas, especially outside Lisbon, Oporto and the Algarve, such as the Alentejo. PEDIP is a special EC programme of aid to develop Portuguese industry.

Business structures
Sociedade Anonima de Responsabilidade Limitada (SA): a public limited company with minimum capital 5 million ESC.
    Sociedade por Quotas de Responsabilidade Limitada (Lda): a private limited company. Minimum capital 400 000 ESC.
    Sociedade en Nome Colectivo (SNC): a partnership, which may be general or limited liability.
    Sole Trader.

Further information
Sue Tyson-Ward, *How to Live & Work in Portugal* (How To Books, 1993). Paperback.

Hints to Exporters: Portugal and *Country Profiles: Portugal* (DTI Export Publications, PO Box 55, Stratford-upon-Avon CV37 9GE. Tel: 0789 296212).

DENMARK

Denmark is one of the smaller, more peaceful and stable countries of the EC—and has been described by one observer as 'as near perfect a country as it is possible to get'. The standard of living is high. The main industries are modern and clean and entrepreneurship is a way of life (Denmark has almost nothing to sell but its ingenuity). It is also a country where small business predominates.

The disadvantages are that Denmark is certainly expensive to live in and set up in. Business is beset by rules and regulations; the Danes have a strong liking for them.

A good many people in Denmark speak English. Although a knowledge of Danish is recommended some expatriate business people get by with only limited knowledge of Danish.

Summary
- good links to both EC and Scandinavian markets
- well educated and trained workforce
- encouragement for clean, high technology industry.

The economy/financial
The economy is characterised by a proliferation of small, efficient business, increasingly dealing in high technology, and aggressively pursuing trade links. As Denmark has no natural resources to speak of it *must* trade overseas to earn a living—something which it has been reasonably successful in doing; 80% of exports are manufactured goods.

Danish economic figures do not however always make good reading. Inflation in the 70s and 80s averaged 8–10%, though is now lower. In the late 1980s growth ran at –1%. The balance of payments has shown a deficit for 30 years (typically 15 billion Kroner).

The banking system is sophisticated and characterised by the availability of substantial mortgage funds. However, venture capital is limited.

Business attitudes
The Danes are hard-working and have a determined attitude towards business. Most businesses are committed to developing overseas trade (as

the home market is so small), irrespective of the Single European Market, or their initial rejection of greater EC union in the 1992 referendum. The quality of life is just as important to most business men and women as money-making.

Main industry/growth areas
There is little heavy industry in Denmark, save some shipbuilding and repair. Fisheries are important. Emphasis is being placed on developing new, environmentally conscious light manufacturing industries. Growth areas are agriculture, food production and processing, alcoholic beverages, chemicals, electronics, textiles, furnishings and some household goods.

Service industries are becoming particularly important. These include shipping, banking, finance, management and business consultancy. Tourist income is important.

Setting up costs
The cost of setting up in Denmark is high, though land and property prices are not the highest in the EC. Staffing costs are likely to be substantial. Conservative estimates are that any given project would require 80%–100% more funding than in the UK.

Geography/suggested locations
Apart from the Jutland peninsula, Denmark consists of a number of islands. Communication with all of them is good; the smaller ones can be isolated but Fyn, Sjaelland, Falster and Lolland all have business and commercial activity. Copenhagen is the only main business centre but there are important centres at Odense and Arhus.

Residence/registration
EC citizens require only a residence permit in order to live in Denmark and establish a business or operate their profession. This should be obtained from the nearest Direktoratet for Udlaendinge (Danish Aliens Department) within three months.

Incorporated companies and limited partnerships must register with the Companies Register (Erhvervs og Selskabsstyrelsen). General partnerships and sole traders usually register also, but it is not compulsory. Tradespeople must register with a professional organisation and lodge surety of 30 000 Kroner. Denmark's insistence that foreign tradespeople speak Danish and are trained to Danish standards contravenes EC laws.

No social security contributions are payable in Denmark and so no social security registration is required.

Lifestyle

The standard of living in Denmark is high; the country has the highest level of weekly spend on food, clothing, and luxuries in the EC. The country is generally very safe, clean and environmentally minded.

However, Denmark is an expensive country in which to live, and not for those on a tight budget. Taxation is very high in order to pay for a very generous social security system. Labour costs are substantial.

Contacts

Newspapers with useful business coverage include *Berlingske Tidende, Den Blå Auis, Politiken, Borsen.*

Royal Danish Embassy
  55 Sloane Street
  London SW1X 9SR
  (071) 333 0200

British Embassy
  Kastelvej 36–40
  2100 Copenhagen
  31 26 46 00

Danish Federation of Small Business
  Amaliegade 15
  1256 Copenhagen
  01 12 36 76

Business data

Government	Coalition

Economy	
Gross Domestic Product	£7 700
Growth	1%
Inflation	4%
VAT	22% single rate
Personal taxation	Up to 78%
Corporation tax	50%

Trade unions
Union activity is considerable but unions are generally not militant. Wages and conditions are negotiated every four years.

Incentives available
Some EC benefits. There are no Danish Government tax incentives to encourage investment. However, non tax incentives include grants, low interest loans, and loan guarantees plus subsidised land. Many are offered by local athorities rather than the Government. There are Development Areas in parts of Jutland, Zealand and Bornholm island.

Business structures
Aktieselskab (A/S): a public limited company with minimum capital of 300 000 Kroner. No limit to the number of shareholders.
Anpartsselskab (ApS): a private limited company. Minimum capital of 80 000 Kroner. Only one shareholder required but may require a Danish promoter.
Interessentskab (I/S): general partnership, unlimited liability.
Kommanditselskab (K/S): limited liability partnership.
Andelsforening/Brugsforening: cooperative society.
Filial af Udenlandsk Selskab: branch of foreign company.
Salgskontor: sales promotion office.
Enkeltmandsvirksomhed: sole trader.

Further information
Hints to Exporters: Denmark and Country Profiles: Denmark (DTI Export Publications, PO Box 55, Stratford-upon-Avon CV37 9GE. Tel: 0789 299212).

LUXEMBOURG

Luxembourg is the smallest state in the EC in geographical terms, but has commercial and light industrial importance disproportionate to its size. In terms of Gross Domestic Product it is also the wealthiest country of the EC (1988: £8 970).

Predominantly, Luxembourg's importance is due to its position at the centre of Europe with immediate access to France, Germany and Belgium. Some firms are set up here to serve all three states. Luxembourg has an independent national identity, but has shared a currency and Customs union with Belgium since 1921—the oldest single market in the world.

Luxembourg is rarely considered the most interesting place to set up. However, the standard of living is high; most people are wealthy. A large proportion of Luxembourg's residents (about 40%) are executive/professional and 27% are foreign. As a result the atmosphere is cosmopolitan and many people are trilingual (French, German and English). Tax laws for non residents are very favourable.

The economy of Luxembourg is sound, but dependent on foreign trade. Manufacturing industries are chiefly plastics, light engineering, electrical equipment, chemicals and textiles. Important services include banking, transport and telecommunications, as well as services supporting the EC 'Eurocrats' who operate here.

Luxembourg welcomes foreign investment and has beneficial corporate tax and company legislation. Both tax and non tax incentives are available including tax exemption and rebates (25% of corporation tax), grants and guaranteed or subsidised loans (up to 4% interest rate subsidy). Labour and establishment costs are high but the productivity rate equals the best in Europe.

EC citizens require only a residence permit in order to live in Luxembourg and establish a business or operate their profession. Businesses should obtain prior approval from the Ministry of Small Firms & Traders, and register with the Registre aux Firmes (Trade Register) at the Tribunal d'Arrondisement (District Court). Registration at the Chamber of Trade is optional, but recommended.

Contacts

Belgo-Luxembourg Chamber of Commerce
36 Piccadilly
London W1Y 9TH
(071) 434 1815

British Chamber of Commerce for Belgium & Luxembourg
30 rue Joseph II
1040 Brussels
2190 788

Embassy of Luxembourg
27 Wilton Crescent
London SW1X 8SD
(071) 235 6961

British Embassy
14 boulevard F.D. Roosevelt
2450 Luxembourg
29864

Chamber of Commerce of the Grand Duchy of Luxembourg
7 rue Alcide de Gasperi
2981 Luxembourg
435853

Board of Economic Development
19–21 boulevard Royal
2910 Luxembourg
4794 231

Ministry of Small Firms & Traders
19–21 boulevard Royal
2910 Luxembourg
4795 517

Further information
Country Profiles: Luxembourg (DTI Export Publications, PO Box 55, Stratford-upon-Avon CV37 9GE. Tel: 0789 296212).

Many sources of information on Belgium also include coverage of Luxembourg.

SWITZERLAND

Switzerland is the smallest yet wealthiest European country outside the EC. At the time of writing the Government has decided to make an application for membership, though applications take at least two years to process, even before accession arrangements commence. So, the benefits and rules of the Single European Market do not apply to Switzerland.

Switzerland has always been an important commercial and business country. Some of the most efficiently run and successful companes in the world are Swiss managed. As a result, however, Switzerland has little need to attract new industry.

Switzerland has long enjoyed a very high standard of living and is a correspondingly expensive country in which to set up and live. Estimates are that setting up costs are 40%–60% higher than other EC countries on average. Favourable company and tax laws are considered to be some incentive, though personal income tax at 25%–34% is not especially low.

Most new business in Switzerland tends to involve high technology manufacturing or services. Growth areas include electronics, computing, pharmaceuticals, high technology chemicals, banking, finance, insurance and business consultancy. Tourism is also important, especially to small business. Entrepreneurs must be fluent in one of the three languages—French, German or Italian—to succeed.

However, the main obstacle to setting up in Switzerland is that as Switzerland is not an EC country all non Swiss nationals need prior consent to settle there. The Swiss Embassy say that:

'As a rule, self-employment is only possible after a Permanent Residence (C-Permit) has been obtained. It is therefore virtually impossible to emigrate to Switzerland for the sole purpose of being self-employed.'

The C Permit (Permanent Residence Permit) is only granted to those who have held a B Permit for 5–10 years. The B Permit is renewable annually and only granted to those who can find employment in Switzerland with an employer who has a quota of work/residence permits issued to him or her by the authorities.

Contacts

Swiss Embassy
    16–18 Montagu Place
    London W1H 2BQ
    (071) 723 0701

British Embassy
    Thunstrasse 50
    3000 Berne
    031 445021

British-Swiss Chamber of Commerce
    Freiestrasse 155
    8032 Zurich

Directorate of British Export Promotion in Switzerland
    Dufourstrasse 56
    8008 Zurich
    01 471520

Further information
Hints to Exporters: Switzerland and *Country Profiles: Switzerland* (DTI Export Publications, PO Box 55, Stratford-upon-Avon CV37 9GE. Tel: 0789 296212).

AUSTRIA

Like its smaller neighbour Switzerland, Austria is somewhat isolated by virtue of the fact that it is not an EC member; Austria has already applied to join the Community, but no decision on accession has yet been reached. Single market benefits and rules do not therefore apply.

Generally, Austria is a more important commercial and industrial country than is often realised. As a German-speaking nation it has strong links with both Switzerland and with Germany; 67% of its trade is with EC countries. It may benefit in future from being so close to the countries of Eastern Europe; 8% of Austrian trade is already with those countries. Austria enjoys a high standard of living, though not as high as in Switzerland or Germany. At least it is not as expensive to set up and live there. Generally the economy is healthy but new business and industry is welcomed, especially those creating links with prospective EC partners. However, company, tax and foreign investment are all subject to complex regulation.

Culturally, Austria is very distinct from its neighbours and those without some further knowledge of this, and of Austrian German, will be at a considerable disadvantage.

Austria does have heavy industry, such as mining and steelworking, which has been subject to some decline. New industries are largely in high technology manufacturing and services; as in Germany some service sectors are very underdeveloped. Start up costs are much in line with those in Germany.

Austria has few major urban areas and most business and commerce, unless connected with tourism, tends to gather in five centres. These are Vienna and to a lesser extent Salzburg, Innsbruck, Linz and Graz.

Those wishing to set up a business or operate a profession in Austria must first obtain a permit from the Provincial Government in the part of Austria in which they wish to establish—these are at Burgenland, Karnten, Niederosterreich, Oberosterreich, Salzburg, Steiermark, Tirol, Vorarlberg and Vienna (Wien). The Austrian authorities are willing to grant permits to foreigners. However, trade and professional people will have to meet Australian standards and acceptance of foreign qualifications may be difficult to achieve.

Contacts

Austrian Embassy
   18 Belgrave Mews West
   London SW1X 5HU
   (071) 235 3731

British Embassy
   Jauresgasse 12
   1030 Vienna
   01 713 1575

Austrian Trade Commission
  1 Hyde Park Gate
  London SW7 5ER
  (071) 584 4411

British Trade Council
  Möllwaldplatz 1/12
  1040 Vienna

Further information
Hints to Exporters: Austria and *Country Profiles: Austria* (DTI Export
Publications, PO Box 55, Stratford-upon-Avon CV37 9GE. Tel: 0789
296212).

NORWAY, SWEDEN, FINLAND

The Scandinavian countries (other than Denmark) are considered much
less by foreigners for the establishment of a new business or branch,
although they have all had success in attracting new service and high technology industries in recent years.

As regards European Community status, Norway was accepted in
1973 but withdrew its application shortly before entering. Sweden has
applied to join the EC but if will be many years before it becomes a full
member, if at all. However, the Scandinavian countries, plus Iceland, have
a partial Single Market already in which trading bureaucracy and barriers
are simplified and there is a Single Market for labour. These matters are
co-ordinated by the Nordic Council, based in Stockholm.

As a result, businesses formed in one country have more open access to
markets in the others. This makes Norway, Sweden or Finland of interest
to business, though Denmark has the advantage of both EC and Scandinavian links. The economy of all the countries is healthy and dependant
on trade between themselves and, principally with the EC. All enjoy a
trade surplus with the UK, but Sweden is by far the most enthusiastic
trading partner; in 1990 £2 712 million of goods were imported from the
UK and £3 594 million exported. 10% of all Sweden's imports came
from the UK.

There is extensive primary industry and some heavy manufacturing in
Scandinavia; these include fisheries, mining, agriculture, timber, motor
manufacture, shipbuilding and repair, chemicals and steel. However, services are a growing sector and these include tourism, computing, electronics, high technology chemicals and transport.

New business is welcomed by all the countries and certain areas (usually the more isolated northern locations) qualify for regional aid and tax and non tax incentives. These are most widespread in Finland; there are no tax incentives in Norway. Subsidised land and reduced payroll tax are offered in every country. Most incentives are available to foreign investors as well as nationals, but foreigners receive no special extra incentives.

Standard of living in all the Scandinavian countries is high; average GDP is £7 900. Living, property and establishment costs exceed the UK by 30%–60%. Rates of personal tax are the highest in Europe (in Sweden 20% national income tax plus 30% municipal income tax). However, corporation tax rates are an incentive to new business—Sweden 30%, Norway 28%, Finland 19%.

Specific consent is required before moving to any of the Scandinavian countries to set up a business. Information should be obtained before you make a decision. Each case is treated on its merits and well prepared plans, based on outside finance and offering local employment potential, are more likely to be accepted. It is important not to set up a non resident business or branch in Scandinavia before making a first application (especially Sweden) as this may cause it to be rejected.

Contacts

Royal Norwegian Embassy
  25 Belgrave Square
  London SW1X 8QD
  (071) 235 7151

British Embassy
  Thomas Heftysgate 8
  0244 Oslo
  02 55 24 00

Finnish Embassy
  38 Chesham Place
  London SW1Y 4RF
  (071) 235 9531

British Embassy
  Itäinen Puistotie
  00140 Helsinki
  90 661293

Swedish Embassy
   11 Montagu Place
   London W1H 2AL
   (071) 724 2101

British Embassy
   Skarpögatan 6
   11527 Stockholm
   08 667 0140

Norwegian Chamber of Commerce
   Norway House
   21–24 Cockspur Street
   London SW1Y 5BN
   (071) 930 0181

Finnish Foreign Trade Association
   Arkadiankatu 4–6B
   00100 Helsinki 10
   90 69591

British-Swedish Chamber of Commerce
   Nybrogatan 75
   511440 Stockholm
   08 665 3425

Swedish Chamber of Commerce for the UK
   72–73 Welbeck Street
   London W1M 7HA
   (071) 935 5487

Further information
The *Hints for Exporters Series* and *Country Profiles Series* both include separate titles on Norway, Sweden and Finland respectively (DTI Export Publications, PO Box 55, Stratford-upon-Avon CV37 9GE. Tel: 0789 296212).

EASTERN EUROPE

Overall potential

The countries of Eastern Europe are still very new to the concept of the market economy. Although most of the countries have been interested in attracting foreign investment for many years—in state partnership projects—only recently has it become possible to open up private businesses in most of them.

So far, foreign investment in Eastern Europe has been steady rather than spectacular. Most foreign businesses in Eastern Europe are branches rather than independent concerns. The consumer economy in these countries is in its infancy. The main attractions to foreigners are cheap land and property, raw materials, and a large supply of labour, often reasonably well trained. But many investors are finding that they can obtain these factors of production in Portugal, Spain, Greece, or even peripheral parts of the UK or Italy at little more cost.

The countries

The countries which have been targeted by investors as having some business potential are the Czech Republic, the Slovak Republic (formerly Czechoslovakia, and part of an alliance known as the Czech and Slovak Federated Republic or CSFR until June 1992), Poland, Hungary and Bulgaria. Romania and the former states of the Soviet Union are still some way from the same level of development. The situation in the former Yugoslavia has become destabilised by war and social breakdown.

Of these, the Czech Republic, Slovak Republic and Poland are receiving closest attention from western entrepreneurs. Poland is most aggressively pursuing free market policies; 900 foreign investment projects were approved in 1989 alone. Czechoslovakia was, in the Iron Curtain days, the most successful Eastern European country economically.

The legal changes to create a free market economy in all the countries were started in 1990 and continue today. Growth in these countries is expected to be strong and all are aiming to have implemented full, free market economies and 'hard' currencies by 1998 at the latest.

Opportunities and costs

One of the main reasons for setting up in Eastern Erope is cost; land and property costs are low, but the cost of establishing basic facilities can be higher. Labour costs are low, but training facilities may be limited. There is little infrastructure. A conservative estimate has put the setting up costs for a manufacturing plant at 60%–70% of those in the UK.

A large proportion of 'new' foreign enterprise in the Czech and Slovak Republics and Poland has consisted of the foreign purchase of enterprises which were previously state owned. This is permitted in most Eastern European countries, although nationals have first call on enterprises chosen for privatisation.

It is difficult to assess the types of business which are being set up, as there is no official information. However, new businesses appear to be largely in manufacturing, particularly low technology manufacturing and basic services. Growth areas include light engineering, assembly work agriculture, food processing, dairy products, motor manufacture, pharmaceuticals, chemicals, printing and tourism. Growth services include accountancy, finance, marketing, management consultancy, real estate, and education (partially operated by private enterprise).

Starting up

All the Eastern European countries are very anxious to attract businesses of all kinds. In all cases approval, including approval to invest, is required by a state agency, such as Poland's Foreign Investment Agency. Certain conditions apply in each country; these are usually less stringent if the business is a foreign branch rather than a resident business. For example, in Poland, the minimum injection of capital into a foreign company setting up as an incorporated company is US$50 000; there is no minimum for a branch. Exchange controls and laws concerning the repatriation of profits exist in all countries.

In all Eastern European countries there are now legal business structures for private enterprise companies, which equate to a private limited company, partnership, and sole trader. For example, in the Czech Republic a private limited company (Společnost s Ručením Omezeným or SRO) requires only one shareholder but a minimum capitalisation of 20 000 Czech Crowns. Both general (Veřejna Obchodní Společnost or VOS) and limited (Komanditní Společnost or KS) partnerships exist.

Before 1990 all the Eastern European countries lacked any commercial law whatsoever. This law continues to evolve and specialist legal and financial advice should be sought. The Eastern European countries are often modelling their Commercial Law Codes on those that exist in the west, rather than on those which existed before the Communist years. For example, all countries impose licensing for certain trades, corporation tax systems, labour and social security laws. Most now allow ownership of private property, but in some places non-nationals may only acquire it on a leasehold basis.

Incentives

As part of their encouragement of foreign investment most Eastern European countries offer incentives for setting up business. Few grants and loans are available from national governments. However, there are both tax and non tax incentives, principally tax incentives. Some examples are:

- Corporation tax exemption (minimum three years in Poland, two years Czech and Slovak Republics).
- Enhanced capital allowances for certain purchases (such as food processing machinery in Poland, 50%).
- Relaxed regulations as to the repatriation of profits.

- Exemption from Customs duties on imports of machinery for an initial period.

- Reduction of rate of income tax applicable to foreign employees (from the standard rate of 32% down to 17% in the Czech Republic, for example).

The European Community also offers assistance to businesses establishing in Eastern Europe. The chief project of interest to businesses is PHARE (**Poland and Hungary Assistance for Restructuring**). Finance is also available through the **European Bank for Reconstruction and Development** (EBRD), mostly for infrastructure and enviromental projects.

Contacts

Further information should be obtained from the respective Embassies and professional advisers at an early stage of planning to set up in Eastern Europe. The regulations are in a constant state of flux and individual cases may be treated on their merits.

Embassy of the Republic of Poland, 47 Portland Place, London W1N 3AG. Tel: (071) 580 4324

British Embassy, 1 Aleja Róz, 00556 Warsaw. Tel: 02 281001

Embassy of the Czech Republic, 25 Kensington Palace Gardens, London W8 4QY. Tel: (071) 229 1255

British Embassy, Thunovská 14, 11800 Prague 1. Tel: 02 533347

European Bank for Reconstruction and Development, 6 Broadgate, London EC2M 2QS. Tel: (071) 496 0060

Polish Chamber of Foreign Trade, PO Box 361, UI Trebacka 4, 00074 Warsaw 2. Tel: 02 602261

Ceskoslovenská Obchodnia Prumyslová Komora, (Czechoslovak Chamber of Commerce & Industry), Argentinska 38, 717005 Prague. Tel: 02 224845

Further information

The *Hints to Exporters Series* includes titles on Bulgaria, Czechoslovakia, Hungary, Poland, Russia and the former Yugoslavia. Check for latest editions in these rapidly-changing areas (DTI Export Publications, PO Box 55, Stratford-upon-Avon CV37 9GE. Tel: 0789 296212).

See also the Kogan Page *Doing Business in Europe Series*, which includes titles on *Hungary, Poland, Czechoslovakia, Romania* and *Bulgaria*, £25 each (Kogan Page, 120 Pentonville Road, London N1 9JN. Tel: 071 278 0433).

Further Information

SUMMARY

1. Further reading — books and directories
   — magazines and journals
2. Useful addresses
3. DTI Regional Offices
4. EuroInfoCentres
5. Key Euro terms & acronyms

1. FURTHER READING

Books

Business Cultures in Europe, Colin Randlesome (Heinemann Professional Publishing)

Buying a Home Abroad, Rebecca Stephens (Sidgwick & Jackson)

The Daily Telegraph Guide to Working Abroad, Godfrey Golzen (Kogan Page)

Doing Business in the European Community, Paul Gibbs (Kogan Page)

Doing Business in the European Community, John Drew (Whurr Publishers, London).

Economist Guides: France, Germany, Italy, Europe City Travel Guide (Hutchinson Business Books)

EEC Brief (Locksley Press Ltd)

The European Community: A Guide to the Maze, S.A. Budd & A. Jones (Kogan Page)

The European Community Fact Book, Alex Rooney (Kogan Page)

France Today, John Ardagh (Penguin)

Germany and the Germans, John Ardagh (Hamilton)

Guide to the Establishment of Enterprises and Craft Businesses in the European Community (Commission of the European Communities) 1990

Harrap's Five Language Business Directory (English, French, German, Italian, Spanish)

How to Get a Job in Europe, Mark Hempshell (How To Books)

How to Get a Job in France, Mark Hempshell (How To Books)

How to Live & Work in Belgium, Marvina Shilling (How To Books)

How to Live & Work in France, Nicole Prevost Logan (How To Books, 2nd edition)

How to Live & Work in Germany, Nessa Loewenthal (How To Books)
How to Live & Work in Italy, Amanda Hinton (How To Books)
How to Live & Work in Portugal, Sue Tyson-Ward (How To Books)
How to Live & Work in Spain, Robert AC Richards (How To Books)
How to Rent & Buy Property in France, Clive Kristen (How To Books, 1993)
How to Rent & Buy Property in Italy, Amanda Hinton (How To Books, 1993)
Living in Portugal, Susan Thackeray (Hale)
The New European Community, Loukas Tsoukalis (Oxford University Press)
1992: The Benefits of a Single Market, Paolo Cecchini (Wildwood House)
1992 Eurospeak Explained, Stephen Crampton (Rosters Ltd)
Operations of the European Community Concerning Small and Medium Sized Enterprises (Commission of the European Communities) 1991
Opportunities in European Financial Services, 1992 and Beyond (John Wiley & Sons)
The Rough Guide Series: France, Greece, Spain, Portugal, Europe, Eastern Europe, Germany, Holland, Belgium & Luxembourg. (Harrap-Columbus)
The Spaniards, J. Hooper (Penguin)
The Times Guide to 1992, Richard Owens & Michael Dynes (Times Books)

Selected DTI Publications
The Single Market: The Facts
Guide to Sources of Advice
Company Law Harmonisation
Europe Open for Professionals
Financial Services
Available from: DTI 1992, PO Box 1992, Cirencester, Gloucestershire GL7 1RN.

Magazines/journals/directories
Chapmans European Directory, Peter Kaye (Chapmans Publishers Ltd)
The European Communities Encyclopaedia and Directory 1992 (Europa Publications)
European Municipal Directory (European Directories Ltd)
The Europe 1992 Directory, A Research and Information Guide (HMSO)
The Expatriate, First Market Intelligence Ltd, 56A Rochester Row, London SW1P 1JU. A monthly magazine covering matters of interest to the expatriate.
Expatxtra, PO Box 300, Jersey C.I. Monthly newsletter for expatriates with much information on financial matters.
Kompass Directories (Kompass Publications). The Kompass directories (published for all main countries) are an authoritative list of industry in that country. Costly to purchase but should be available at all main libraries.
Resident Abroad, 102–108 Clerkenwell Road, London EC1M 5SA. Tel: (071) 251 9321. Monthly magazine for expatriates giving much financial advice.

2. USEFUL ADDRESSES

Association of British Chambers of Commerce, 9 Tufton Street, London SW1. Tel: (071) 222 1555.
Association of Language Export Centres, PO Box 1574, London NW1 4NJ. Tel: (071) 224 3748.

Barclays Bank Plc, Expatriate Dept, 13 Library Place, St Helier, Jersey. Tel: (0534) 26145.

Berlitz International, 79 Wells Street, London W1A 3BZ. Tel: (071) 637 0330.

British Association of Removers, 3 Churchill Court, 58 Station Road, North Harrow, Middlesex HA2 7SA. Tel: (081) 861 3331.

British Bankers Association, 10 Lombard Street, London EC3 9EL. Tel: (071) 623 4001.

BSI Enquiry Services, Linford Wood, Milton Keynes, Bucks MK14 6LE. Tel: (0908) 221166.

BUPA International Sales Office, Provident House, Essex St, London WC2R 3AX.

Centre for International Briefing, Farnham Castle, Surrey GU9 0AG. Tel: (0252) 7-1194

Commission of the European Communities, 8 Storey's Gate, London SW1P 3AT. Tel: (071) 973 1992.
Also:
9 Alva Street, Edinburgh EH2 4PH. Tel: (031) 225 2058.
4 Cathedral Road, Cardiff CF1 9SG. Tel: (0222) 371631.
9/15 Bedford Street, Belfast BT2 7EG. Tel: (0232) 240708.
200 rue de la Loi, 1049 Brussels.

Council of British Independent Schools in the European Community (COBISEC), Chaussée de Louvain, Tervuren, 1980 Brussels. Tel: 02 767 47 00.

Council of the European Communities, 170 rue de la Loi, 1048 Brussels. Tel: 02 234 61 11.

Department of Social Security Overseas Branch, Newcastle upon Tyne NE98 1YX.

Department of Trade & Industry (DTI), 1 Victoria Street, London SW1H 0ET. Tel: (071) 215 5000.

ECIS (European Council of International Schools) 21B Lavant Street, Petersfield, Hants GU32 3EW. Tel: (0230) 68244.

Employment Conditions Abroad Ltd, Anchor House, 10 Britten Street, London SW3 3TY. Tel: (071) 351 7151.

Employment Department, Qualifications and Standards Branch, Room E303, Moorfoot, Sheffield S1 4PQ. Tel: (0742) 594144.

Euro-link for Lawyers, Greatminster House, Lister Hill, Horsforth, Leeds LS18 5DL. Tel: (0532) 581638.

European Bank for Reconstruction and Development, 6 Broadgate, London EC2M 2QS. Tel: (071) 496 0060.

European Investment Bank, 68 Pall Mall, London SW1Y 5ES. Tel: (071) 839 3351.

European Venture Capital Association, Keiberpark 6, Box 6, 1930 Zaventem. Tel: 02 720 60 10.

Export Market Information Centre (EMIC), Ashdown House, 123 Victoria Street, London SW1E 6RB. Tel: (071) 215 5444.

Exports to Europe Branch (DTI), Bay 956, Kingsgate House, 66–74 Victoria Street, London SW1E 6SW.

Financial Services Division (DTI), 10–18 Victoria Street, London SW1H 0NN.

Independent Schools Information Service (ISIS), 56 Buckingham Gate, London SW1E 6AG. Tel: (071) 630 8793.

Inland Revenue Claims Branch, Merton Road, Bootle L69 9BL.

Linguaphone, 124 Brompton Road, London SW3 2TL.

Lloyds Bank Plc, Isle of Man Expatriate Centre, 7–11 Douglas St, Peel, Isle of Man. Tel: (0624) 844051.

Midland Bank Plc, Expatriate Dept, 8 Library Place, St Helier, Jersey.

Natwest Expatriate Service, PO Box 12, 6 High Street, Chelmsford, Essex CM1 1BL. Tel: (0245) 261891.

Official Journal of the European Communities, available from HMSO, 51 Nine Elms Lane, London SW8 5DR. Tel: (071) 873 9090.

Passport Office, Clive House, 70 Petty France, London SW1H 9HD.

Technical Help to Exporters (THE), Linford Wood, Milton Keynes. Bucks MK14 6LE. Tel: (0908) 220022.

The Employment Service, Steel City House, c/o Moorfoot, Sheffield S1 4PQ. Tel: (0742) 753275.

The European Parliament (London Office), 2 Queen Anne's Gate, London SW1H 9AA. Tel: (071) 222 0411.

The Law Society of England & Wales, 50 Chancery Lane, London WC2A 1SX. Tel: (071) 320 5673.

The Law Society of Scotland, 26 Drumsneugh Gardens, Edinburgh EH3 7YR. Tel: (031) 226 741.

3. DEPARTMENT OF TRADE & INDUSTRY REGIONAL OFFICES

DTI General Enqiries—(071) 215 5000

In England
DTI North East
  Newcastle Upon Tyne
  (091) 232 4722
DTI North West
  Manchester
  (061) 838 5000
  and Liverpool
  (051) 224 6300
DTI Yorkshire & Humberside
  Leeds
  (0532) 443171
  DTI East Midlands
  Nottingham
  (0602) 506181
DTI West Midlands
  Birmingham
  (021) 212 5000
DTI East
  Cambridge
  (0223) 461939
DTI South East
  London
  (071) 215 0574
  and Reading
  (0734) 395600

and Reigate
(0737) 226900
DTI South West
Bristol
(0272) 272666

In Scotland
Industry Department for Scotland
Glasgow
(041) 248 4774
Enterprise Services Scotland Ltd
Edinburgh
(031) 346 9170

In Wales
Welsh Office
Cardiff
(0222) 825097

In Northern Ireland
Industrial Development Board for Northern Ireland
Belfast
(0232) 233233

4. EUROINFOCENTRES (EICs)—EUROPEAN INFORMATION CENTRES

Belfast
EuroInfoCentre, Local Enterprise Development Unit, LEDU House, Upper Galway, Belfast BT8 4TB. Tel: (0232) 491031. Contact: Eleanor Butterwick.

Birmingham
Chamber of Commerce, 75 Harborne Road, PO Box 360, Birmingham B15 3DH. Tel: (021) 454 6171. Contact: Sharon Clift.

Bradford
West Yorkshire European Business Information Centre, Bradford Enterprise Centre, Britannia House, Broadway, Bradford BD1 1JF. Tel: (0274) 754262. Contact: Mohan da Silva.

Brighton
EuroInfoCentre, Federation of Sussex Industries and Chamber of Commerce, Seven Dials, Brighton BN1 3JS. Tel: (0273) 220870. Contact: John Thum.
Bristol
EuroInfoCentre, Bristol Chamber of Commerce & Industry, 16 Clifton Park, Bristol BS8 3BY. Tel: (0272) 737373. Contact: Sharon Copper.

Cardiff
EuroInfoCentre, UWCC—Guest Building, PO Box 430, Cardiff CF1 3XT. Tel: (0222) 229525. Contact: Brian Wilcox.

Exeter
EuroInfoCentre South West, Exeter Enterprises Ltd., Hailey Wing, Reed Hall, Univesity of Exeter, Exeter EX4 4QR. Tel: (0392) 214085. Contact: Diana Letcher.

Glasgow
EuroInfoCentre, Scottish Development Agency, Atrium Court, 50 Waterloo Street, Glasgow G2 6HQ. Tel: (041) 221 0999. Contact: Catherine Smith.

Hull
EuroInfoCentre, Brynmor Jones Library, University of Hull, Cottingham Road, Hull HU6 7RX. Tel: (0482) 465940. Contact: Freda Carrol.

Inverness
EuroInfoCentre, Highland Opportunity Ltd, Development Dept, Highland Regional Council, Regional Buildings, Glenuquart Road, Inverness IV3 5NX. Tel: (0463) 234121. Contact: Hugh Black.

Leeds
Mid Yorkshire EuroInfoCentre, Leeds Polytechnic Library, Calverley Street, Leeds LS1 3HE. Tel: (0532) 832600 extension 3845. Contact: Meg Gardiner.

Leicester
EuroInfoCentre, Euro Team Business Advice Centre, 30 New Walk, Leicester LE1 6TF. Tel: (0533) 554464. Contact: Michael Coyne.

Liverpool
EuroInfoCentre North West, Liverpool City Libraries, William Brown Street, Liverpool L3 8EW. Tel: (051) 298 1928. Contact: Howard Patterson.

London (1)
EuroInfoCentre, London Chamber of Commerce & Industry, 69 Cannon Street, London. EC4N 5AB. Tel: (071) 489 1992. Contact: Beth Reyney.

London (2)
EuroInfoCentre, Small Firms Service, 11 Belgrave Road, London SW1V 1RB. Tel: (071) 828 6201. Contact: Steven Elliot.

Maidstone
EuroInfoCentre, Kent County Council, Springfield, Maidstone. Kent. ME14 2LL. Tel: (0662) 696130. Contact: David Oxlade.

Manchester
EuroInfoCentre, Chamber of Commerce & Industry, 56 Oxford Street, Manchester M60 7HJ. Tel: (061) 236 3210. Contact: Steven Atkinson.

Mold
EuroInfoCentre, Library & Information Service, County Civic Centre, Mold CH7 6NW. Tel: (0352) 2121 Extension 2494. Contact: Eric Davies.

Newcastle upon Tyne (1)
North of England EuroInfoCentre, Northern Development Company, Great North House, Sandyford Road, Newcastle upon Tyne NE1 8ST. Tel: (091) 261 0026. Contact: Marion Schooler.

Newcastle upon Tyne (2)
North of England EuroInfoCentre, European Documentation Centre, Polytechnic Library, Elison Building, Newcastle Upon Tyne NE1 8ST. Tel: (091) 261 5131. Contact: Anne Ramsay.

Norwich
Chamber of Commerce & Industry, 112 Barrack Road, Norwich NR3 1UB. Tel: (0603) 625977. Contact: Sarah Jane Abercrombie.

Nottingham
EuroInfoCentre, CCI South Block, Harley House Industrial Estate, Haydn Road, Sherwood, Nottingham. Tel: (0602) 222414. Contact: Anne Pearce.

Sheffield
South Yorkshire EuroInfoCentre, Sheffield Polytechnic Library, Pond Street, Sheffield S1 1WB. Tel: (0742) 532126. Contact: Graham Wills.

Slough
EuroInfoCentre, Thames-Chiltern Chamber of Commerce & Industry, Commerce House, Bath Road, Slough SL1 3SB. Tel: (0753) 77877. Contact: Julia Rees.

Southampton
EuroInfoCentre, Central Library, Civic Centre, Southampton SO9 4XF. Tel: (0703) 832866. Contact: David Dance.

Stafford
EuroInfoCentre, Staffordshire Development Association, 3 Martin Street, Stafford ST16 2LH. Tel: (0785) 59528. Contact: Nicola Adamson.

Telford
EuroInfoCentre, Shropshire Chamber of Commerce & Industry, Industry House, 16 Halesfield, Telford TF7 4TA. Tel: (0952) 588766. Contact: Robert Trustlove.

5. KEY EURO TERMS AND ACRONYMS

Approximation—The collection of a range of diverse issues into defined groups (EC policy technique).
BC-NET—Business Co-Operation Network.
CEN—European Committee for Standards (French abbreviation).
CENELEC—European Committee for Electrotechnical Standardisation (French abbreviation).

Consultation Procedure—An EC procedure which allows the European Parliament one reading of a proposal before it is adopted as an EC law.

CPC—Community Patent Convention.

Craft Business—Usually taken to refer to a trade business with under 10 employees.

CTM—Community Trademark.

Directive—A legally binding EC proclamation which member states must incorporate into their own law by national Act of Parliament.

Decision—An order made, under existing EC law, by an EC authority. A statutory instrument.

DG—Directorate General. There are 23 DGs or departments in the Commission of the European Communities.

EAGGF—European Agricultural Guidance and Guarantee Fund.

EBRD—European Bank for Reconstruction and Development.

ECJ—European Court of Justice.

Ecu—The European Currency Unit, a currency valued by reference to all 12 of the Community currencies. The unit which is used in all official budgets and expenditure plans.

EEB—Exports to Europe Branch (of the DTI).

EEIG—European Economic Interest Grouping. A new cross-border EC business structure.

EFTA—European Free Trade Association. Comprises Austria, Finland, Iceland, Norway, Sweden, Switzerland.

EIB—European Investment Bank.

EIC's—European Information Centres, also known as EuroInfoCentres.

EMIC—Export Market Information Centre (DTI).

EMS—European Monetary System. A system for stabilising exchange rates between EC countries.

EMU—Economic Monetary Union. The proposed adoption of uniform EC economic and monetary policy.

EP—European Parliament.

EPC—European Patent Convention.

ERDF—European Research and Development Fund.

ESF—European Social Fund.

EVCA—European Venture Capital Association.

Harmonise/Harmonisation—To make a law or procedure meet the same or a similar standard in all EC countries. Usually achieved by an EC body examining current law and practice in each of the 12 EC states and then the introduction of a regulation or directive to develop or replace existing laws or standards by a common arrangement.

Harmonised—A law or area of practice which has, to date, been rendered the same or similar in all EC countries by an EC regulation or directive. For example, certain aspects of Company Law.

IMP—Integrated Mediterranean Programme. A programme of development targeted at the Mediterranean EC countries.

Mutual recognition—A practice by which a member state agrees to adopt certain measures which apply in other EC members, even where there are differences between the law in both countries. For example, the mutual recognition of qualifications.

OJ—Official Journal (of the European Communities). Where most legislation and official information is announced.

PHARE—Poland and Hungary Assistance for Economic Restructuring (French abbreviation).

Reciprocity—An arrangement under which non EC companies can do business in the EC on the same terms as EC companies can in non EC countries.

Regulations (EC)—Once issued EC regulations are legally binding throughout the EC, without any requirement to write them into national law.

SE—Societas Europea, a new European company structure.

SEA—Single European Act. The legislation, signed by EC members in 1986, which created the Single European Market.

SEM—Single European Market. A situation whereby companies and individuals in one EC country can trade with their counterparts in other countries without the hindrance of intra-national barriers.

SME—Small and Medium Sized Enterprise. Generally taken as a business employing less than 500 people.

State aids—Government grants and loans.

Subsidiarity—The principle whereby EC legislation is broadly drafted thus permitting individual member states to add the fine detail.

Index